TALES OF LOVING AND LEAVING

➤◄ AND ➤◄

Gaby Weiner

authorHOUSE®

AuthorHouse™ UK
1663 Liberty Drive
Bloomington, IN 47403 USA
www.authorhouse.co.uk
Phone: 0800.197.4150

Published by AuthorHouse   09/12/2016

ISBN: 978-1-5246-3508-4 (sc)
ISBN: 978-1-5246-3509-1 (hc)
ISBN: 978-1-5246-3507-7 (e)

CONTENTS

Frocht family tree

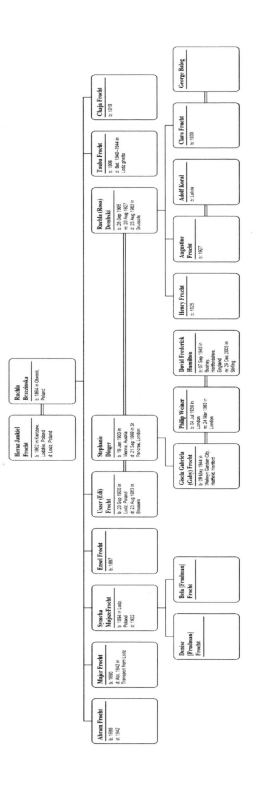

Herzл Jankiel Frocht
b: 1862 in Warszaw, Łódzkie, Poland
d: Łódz, Poland

Ruchla Brzezinska
b: 1864 in Oharock, Poland

Abram Frocht
b: 1898
d: 1942

Majer Frocht
b: 1890
d: Abt. 1942 in Transport from Lodz

Symcha Majսer Frocht
b: 1894 in Lodz, Poland
d: 1922

Ensel Frocht
b: 1897

Uszer (Edi) Frocht
b: 20 Sep 1900 in Lodz, Poland
d: 23 Aug 1983 in Brussels

Stephanie Dinger
b: 19 Jan 1903 in Vienna, Austria
d: 21 Sep 1988 in St Pancras, London

Ruchla (Rosa) Dembski
b: 28 Sep 1905
m: 20 Aug 1927
d: 23 Aug 1963 in Brussels

Tauba Frocht
b: 1906
d: Bet. 1940–1944 in Lodz ghetto

Chaja Frocht
b: 1919

Denise [Freulman] Frocht

Bela [Freulman] Frocht

Gisela Gabriela (Gaby) Frocht
b: 09 May 1944 in Welwyn Garden City, Hatfield, Hertford

Philip Weiner
b: 04 Jul 1939 in London
m: 24 Mar 1963 in London

David Frederick Hamilton
b: 07 Sep 1943 in Bushey, Hertfordshire, England
m: 29 Dec 2005 in Stirling

Henry Frocht
b: 1925

Augustine Frocht
b: 1927

Adolf Koral
b: Latvia

Clara Frocht
b: 1930

George Balog

Dinger family tree

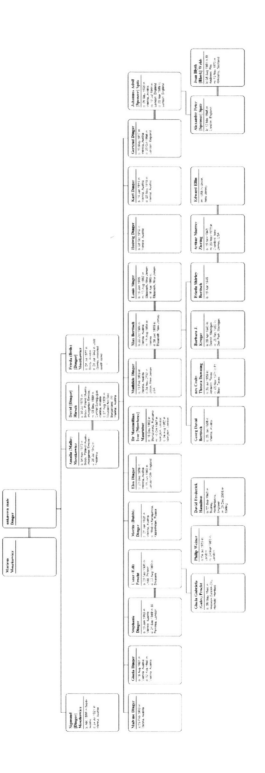

ACKNOWLEDGEMENTS

This book has been a long time in coming to fruition. I had long pondered how I might find out more about my mother and her sisters, who came to London from Vienna in December 1938, just before war started. I had a few documents and several photograph albums but not much more. I was reminded that, if I didn't do something soon, everyone who had known them would be dead; so began my long journey to find long-lost relatives and distant relations and to tell the family story. In so doing, the story-line changed many times, largely due to the generosity and Candour of people that I talked with, wrote to, emailed, messaged, phoned or otherwise harangued. Without them, there would be no book!

I would like to thank them all, but in particular, Chimen Abramsky, Charmian Brinson, Miriam David, Sue Davidson, Judy Dean, Frank Feiner, Irina Isaakyan, Anna Izykowska, Patricia Krus, Martin Lawn, Danny Lesser, Geraldine Locise, Jenny Ozga, Anna Paczuska, Caroline Pick, Leen Preesman and Ruth Thomson.

Members of my wider family who helped me on my way include Carin, Clara and Claude Balog; George Bertish; Augustine and Yves Koral; Amalia Michaels; Alec Spencer; John Spencer; Daniel, Saira, and Philip Weiner; and Arthur and Freda Ziering.

I wish to give particular thanks also to Michael Erben, Gill Clarke, Zoe Parker, and other members of the British Sociological Association Auto/Biography Study Group, who patiently listened to my yearly presentations and offered me much good advice. I am also indebted to David Hamilton for his encouragement, patience, and support throughout the decade or so of research and writing on this project and especially for enabling me to locate and visit the Belgian part of my family.

Gaby Weiner

Tell ye your children of it
and let your children tell their children,
and their children another generation.
—Joel 1:3

In many ways…the completeness of biography, …. is an ironic fiction,
since no life can ever be known completely, nor would we want to
know every fact about an individual….. The 'plot' of a biography is
superficially based on the birth, life, and death of the subject; 'character',
in the vision of the author. Both are as much creations of the biographer,
as they are of a novelist. We content ourselves with 'authorized fictions'.
—Ira Bruce Nadel, *Biography: Fiction, Fact & Form*, 1986

INTRODUCTION

The stories of so-called ordinary families and their place in history are important, as E. P. Thompson showed more than half a century ago in his magisterial *The Making of the English Working Class*[1]. They are not the stuff of kings and queens or governments or wars, even though these inevitably affect them. More importantly perhaps, they throw light on how political movements and decisions affect ordinary individuals and, as fascinating, how those individuals react to those decisions.

But who is to write such stories? Historians generally take their topics from society's main actors or from gaps that need filling by or questions posed to a particular historical field. With notable exceptions[2], historians have found it difficult to give attention to the materials needed to reveal the landscape of ordinary lives. As a result, compiling and telling these kinds of stories are left to those who have a special interest, for example, family members – hence, my interest in narrating these three lives and my concern to find as much as I can about them. This interest is shared with only a few others, perhaps my family and friends, especially those closest, such as my own children, Daniel and Saira, who have expressed interest and sometimes pride in what I have been doing. Others have shown curiosity about one aspect or another or about the unusualness or uniqueness or historical importance of the story or stories I tell. I am, however, the one person who has had the time and resolve to do the research; to search out informants, websites, and archives; to visit places and spaces; and to cross continents, languages, and time.

I also sense that, If I do not bring them to life now, the opportunity to turn the spotlight on these ostensibly ordinary people who were, in fact, extraordinary will be lost.

A main task for mainstream historians (after, one imagines, seeking out accuracy and truth) is to make the sometimes dry bones of history appealing to the would-be reader. This is even more of a problem for those writing about the ordinary and commonplace. An abiding concern of mine has, therefore, been how to make the lives of my maternal grandmother, Amalia Dinger; my mother, Stefanie Dinger/Frocht; and my father, Uszer Frucht, attractive to those outside the family circle. What aspects of their lives might best interest the reader? Can I somehow spice up the central love affair? Might involvement of the secret services be more appealing? Should I place most emphasis on the mystery and secrets surrounding the main protagonists?

Another quandary has been where I place myself in the narrative. If, as already suggested, commitment to revealing ordinary people's stories comes mainly from those closest to them, it is for a reason. As daughter and granddaughter, I am closely connected to the lives told – which relate to *my* history, *my* identity, *my* personhood. It is through me and through my physicality and my familial positioning that the three lives come together. Yet, despite my centrality to the book, I have sought to absent myself from the text; I do not want this book to be about me.

This has created a dilemma since, as I attempt to recount one or more of these lives, the 'I' inevitably emerges. Where the narration has taken place in public (for instance, at a seminar or conference) someone generally wants to know where I fit in and what my motivation is in researching and writing about these lives. Whilst this has challenged my resolve to take myself out of the text, it has also enabled me to acknowledge the effects that this journey back in history has had on me. For example, the memory of the pinch of pain I felt suddenly and unexpectedly on first seeing my father's wife's grave – rather than my mother's – alongside his.

So I have sought to use the 'I' word sparingly but find it unavoidable in reflecting on why I have written this book now and why it has emerged in this particular form. Indeed, why spend so much time on these three lives? There have been so many books written already about the Holocaust; is another one really necessary? Surely, as some have said to me, 'We have seen and heard enough.'[3]

I have my reasons for wanting (even *needing*) to narrate this story. First, my mother was the first and perhaps the most important influence on me and on the person I have become. She died in 1969, nearly half a century ago. I have almost forgotten what she looked like, although I see her again and again through the photographs, letters, and documents that she left behind. My favourite photograph of her was taken sometime in the 1940s when she was in her early forties.

Here she is as I envisage her – beautiful, soft, warm, intelligent, and increasingly more a historical than personal figure. Although I lived with her for twenty-five years – from my birth until her death – I remember little. I can recall earlier memories – of me as a child in the bath imagining myself an adult with our roles reversed and then of me bathing my mother. I remember the excitement and dread when my father was due to arrive. I remember being very small and clinging to her hand on a Saturday afternoon, looking up at a crowd of Arsenal supporters going off to a football match. I remember her ritual of finishing the ironing on New Year's Eve and so on. Later memories are less detailed, so one aim of this book is to draw on a variety of sources, including the memories and accounts of others, to provide a more rounded portrait of my mother, one that I can revisit and recapture whenever I want to.

Other reasons for the book are more political. I have written this book as an act of restitution, to give voice to people like my mother, father, and grandmother, who were harassed and maltreated during their lifetime and who may at last be granted dignity and affirmation. I also aim to explore the human consequences of a regime of horror and its effects on a particular group of people, who happened to be Jewish and who happened to be members of my family. By telling the stories of these particular individuals, I want to personalise what we now call the Holocaust (but what my mother referred to as 'Hitler'[4]). I also seek to show the effects of separation and trauma and explore how ordinary human beings respond when confronted by horror – they get on with life, go on to make different futures, and seek to be ordinary again. Becoming 'ordinary' in a new country is the aim of most refugees, and it is what I most wanted as an adolescent – despite (or because of) my strange name and foreign-sounding relatives. I also want to show that, out of the numbers and numbers and numbers of people wiped out by the Nazi-led genocide (as well as those others whose lives were damaged irretrievably as a result), myths were created, secrets were perpetuated, lies were told, shelter was found, and futures were shaped.

So my intentions are to rescue these three so-called ordinary people from the invisibility into which they have been cast by the grand narratives of political and social histories of war and displacement and to restore them to their rightful place in the histories of migration, settlement, and achievement. Their lives were shaped by not only Nazism but also other great events of the twentieth century, including the Russian Revolution; scientific, technological, and artistic developments; and the displacement and migration of millions following two world wars – as well as by heroism; bravery; and, dare I say, love. The stories I want to tell are hopeful as well as tragic.

My aim originally was to write an 'academic' book because it is a genre of which I have experience and because it lends itself relatively easily to the materials that I have accumulated. In this first envisioning, I aimed to explore the extent to which first-generation migrants share certain experiences, not only in the past, but today. I wanted to show how my mother and her two sisters suffered trauma, poverty, and poor health arising from their refugee experience, and also how they recreated their lives, the extent of their gratitude to their eventual country of domicile (Britain), and their aspirations for their offspring, from which I have personally benefited.

However, in carrying out my investigations, I uncovered a multiplicity of stories about my father as well as my mother, which revealed not only the sad ends of many in their immediate families but also, less expectedly, scandals and secrets within the family and the malevolent impact of state bureaucracies and surveillance cultures of wartime Europe and post-war Britain. The familiar immigrant story of exile, uncertainty, and eventual settlement has been shattered into pieces, each piece constituting a story in itself. How could I identify what the Swedes call a 'red thread' in my story or stories? What overall message might I want to convey? What explanation might I want to offer? Creating coherence around telling the stories of three people's lives, which covered a century or more, seemed a possible way forward.

I decided, in the end, not to go down the academic road but to tell new stories – not only as a contribution to history with a capital 'H', but also so that my children and their children and their children's children and others too could gain a sense of how they got to be the people they are. In writing for them, I sense a wider audience to stand as witness of – and to gain insight into – the past. Of course, it is impossible for me to recreate the past with any degree of certainty or to describe what people long ago felt or if and why they acted in certain ways. So, like many others in such circumstances, I have sought to fill the gaps by drawing on other people's stories and recounted experiences of the same period and from the same places.

As already noted, at the heart of the stories and at the centre of the investigation circle lie three people – my maternal grandmother, Amalia Moszkowicz Dinger; my mother, Steffi Dinger; and my father, Uszer Frocht. My birth, towards the end of the war, serves as a bridge to the separate lives. All I had initially were documents left by my mother and two of her sisters – birth certificates and exit documents, mostly in German, and other personal effects, such as photographs, correspondence, medical records, and accounts. There was little on or from my father – just some photographs and a few short handwritten letters. The circle widened as I discovered the existence of official records for both parents – in Britain, where my mother lived from 1938 onwards, and in Belgium, where my father lived for most of his life.

My mother's failed applications for British naturalisation (or citizenship as we call it today) in the 1950s meant that she had much more 'official' documentation on her, when compared with her two sisters, Elsa and Trude, who became British subjects more or less automatically in the late 1940s, following the naturalisation of their husbands. The rejection of my mother's citizenship applications led, I am sure, to much distress at the time. But I have reaped the rewards by being able to read a bulging file on her, now in the National Archive at Kew. My mother's continued 'alien' status also meant that she was obliged to inform the police of any change in job or address, and this record has provided me with another rich source of information. Moreover, as a Jewish refugee in Britain in the late 1930s, her life was ruled by bodies such as the German Jewish Aid Committee (GJAC), which were not only responsible for organising the rescue of many Jews from Europe during the Nazi period but which also took care of and kept information on the individual Jews who stayed. So ironically, her failure to achieve the British citizenship she so desired in order to keep herself and her daughter safe has ensured that papers exist on her today that would otherwise have been destroyed. Therefore, a more detailed version of her story can now be told.

In contrast, I drew a blank regarding records and information on my father's relatively short sojourn in England between 1938 and 1946, excepting a couple of references to him in sources related to Jewish activism in London in the wartime period. A letter from the

Home Office in response to my enquiry indicated that the file that had been held on him had been destroyed long ago. I thought that I had reached a dead end. But fortune intervened.

I was asked to do some work in Brussels, where my father lived after leaving Britain, and I took the opportunity while there to see whether I could find anything more about him. I knew that he had arrived in Belgium first as an migrant from Poland in the 1920s and later as a deportee from Britain in 1946. I knew also that most governments, whatever time and place, expend considerable energy in keeping a close watch on their immigrants. Belgium proved exemplary in this respect, and I managed, with help, to locate a substantial file on him in the immigrant section (Police D'Etranger) of the national archive in Brussels. This was an enormously satisfying moment for me – to see my father, hitherto an ephemeral and opaque presence in my life, 'fixed' in time and place.

The file covers the period from Uszer Frucht's arrival via Germany as a miner in 1923 aged twenty-three to his eventual expulsion from Belgium in 1938 and then from 1946, when he returned to Belgium from Britain, until 1974, when he achieved full Belgian citizenship. The record ceases then, although he lived for a further six or seven years. The file, 279 pages in length, contains a variety of documents, among them applications for identity cards, change of address details, documentation on his official expulsion from Belgium in 1938, and details of his efforts to return before and after the War. I was fortunate in being able to arrange for a digital copy of the file to be made and sent to me, so that I could work on it at home.

A particular problem vis-à-vis the Belgian file was translation and interpretation. The main languages of the file are French and Flemish, and my first and probably only good language knowledge is English, although I retain a smattering of schoolgirl French. Nevertheless, I have blundered on and tried to translate the whole file, with the help of a Flemish-speaking friend and numerous dictionaries, both in book form and on the Internet.

For my maternal grandmother, Amalia Dinger, there was hardly anything at all, save a couple of small snapshots in my mother's possession, a letter of condolence from the Red Cross on her death, and a few details about her in the Vad Yashem Holocaust listing of the dead.

In order to gain a more personal dimension, I added to this database of documentation interviews with and visits to various family members and friends who had personally known my mother and/or father, although, inevitably, there were relatively few some four decades after the main events of my parents' story. An interview carried out in 1986 with John Spencer, husband of my mother's sister Trude when he was eighty, proved exceptionally insightful, as he offered what might be called a frank 'insider' perspective on our 'unusual' family circumstances, as well as on what it meant to be a refugee in wartime. My mother and her two sisters died in the 1960s, and though my father survived until 1980, I lost touch with him in his last decade, following my mother's death – so, except for some personal letters, their voices and perspectives are missing.

Moreover, putting together the material for the book has utilised the range of skills I developed as an academic and researcher. It has involved, for example, interviewing, accessing archives and records, reviewing background literature, and so on. Notwithstanding, the problems that have emerged have been many, primarily due the huge canvas on which my familial story has been played out. I have drawn on a multiplicity of sources of information for the crafting of *Tales of Loving and Leaving* including, but not limited to, general histories of Poland, Russia, Belgium, and the UK; histories of the Jewish peoples in these countries and elsewhere; histories of war, displacement, and migration; archives from across the world containing documents in Yiddish, Hebrew, Polish, Flemish, French, German, and English; memoirs, biographies, autobiographies, and accounts by and of survivors, immigrants, and refugees; and a multitude of websites, databases, records, and registers.

Places and spaces have also been a magnet for time and energy. For example, I've sought out family origins in the Ukraine, Poland, and Austria and visited relatives in the United States of America and Belgium. In these disparate places, I located, identified, and accessed records; visited local and national archives; and interviewed and spoke with people who perhaps knew something or knew someone who knew more. And so the list goes on. And still, large gaps remain, which require imagination and creativity to circumvent. Indeed, I could go on researching forever, chasing up the latest book, website, or source that might illuminate the circumstances in which my maternal grandmother, mother, father, or one or another of their contemporaries acted or were acted upon at a particular place and time.

An illustration of the detail involved concerns a minor character known to my father while he was living in London during the war. Chimen Abramsky had written a chapter in a Yiddish-language book with which my father was associated. I found the book, which celebrated the twenty-fifth anniversary of the Russian Revolution, in a name search on my father in the British Library. After some investigation, I found out that Chimen was still alive and living in London and wrote to him requesting an interview. By return, I received a kindly response written in a wobbly hand confirming that Chimen had indeed known of my father's existence but had not met him personally. He declined my offer of a visit, explaining that, since he was now ninety years old, he was not up to receiving visitors. So this line of enquiry fizzled out – until, in 2010, Chimen's obituary appeared in *The Guardian* newspaper. I learnt that Chimen Abramsky had been a Russian-born Jewish intellectual, historian, book collector, and bibliographer of world renown; that he had never attended school and had been educated at home in Yiddish, Russian, and Hebrew; that he secretly cultivated a lifelong interest in Karl Marx; and that he ended his years training a generation of Jewish scholars in Oxford and London Universities.

More recently, a friend found a biography of Chimen written in 2014 by his grandson Sasha Abramsky, *The House of Twenty Thousand Books*. It told of the library Chimen had accumulated, which combined, as the book jacket describes, 'the exuberant, passionate jostling of two traditions – Jewish and Marxist', which were incidentally also the predominant traditions of my father. I learnt that Chimen

Abramsky had rubbed shoulders with the good and the great of the two traditions, among them, Isaiah Berlin, Chaim Herzog, and latterly Tariq Ali. These and many others received a mention in the book. My father, though, did not, as far as I could see. There was no index to the book, so I could not look him up. So questions surfaced: How much time should I invest in reading this book? Was it likely to reveal further insights into my father's life? Might it provide more background? Or would it be just one more cul-de-sac resulting in a depletion of time and energy?

I ventured to reread Chimen's original letter to me and understood for the first time my father's association in London with, or even leadership of, a body called the Jewish Cultural Club (JCC) (with which he shared an address). According to Chimen's letter, JCC consisted of, 'Polish Jews, escaping from Occupied Europe...who were communists or close to communists'. This led me to a description of the activities of the JCC in Henry Srebrnik's book *London Jews and British Communism 1935–1945*[5]:

> The JCC...had its origins in a group of Eastern European Jews who had come to Britain from Belgium and France after the fall of France... The JCC reprinted appeals from the Jewish Anti-Fascist Committee, often adding its own urgent commentary... In November 1942, the JCC commemorated the Russian Revolution of 1917 by publishing *25 Yor Sovyetn Farband* (*25 Years of the Soviet Union*) ... The JCC also circulated appeals for aid to the USSR and announcements of conferences, such as the one held in March 1943 to celebrate the twenty-fifth anniversary of the Red Army.

So here was confirmation, if one was needed, of the source of the book in which my father is named as editor. As Chimen informed me in his letter, 'In 1942 the Jewish Cultural Club under my [Chimen's] responsibility decided to issue a miscellany dedicated to twenty-five years of Soviet power...[which] gathered round it some of the best Yiddish scholars in England and in the Soviet Union.' My father's connection to the publication was primarily bureaucratic; while not a scholar, his name and address were needed due to the wartime requirement for all journals and miscellaneous publications to include details of production and organisation. Chimen wrote, 'We needed an address and a name of a proprietor.' As a consequence, and several hundred pages and some weeks later, I was able to clear up a minor correction to my father's place in British communism.

Sources that have been particularly helpful in locating the interlinking stories of the three lives in space and time are my old stalwart friends – books. I consulted tomes of a great and diverse range of authorship. Included are those of the most eminent of scholars and historians of the period, such as Hannah Arendt, Arthur Koestler, Eric Hobsbawm, and Tony Judt. I've turned to British specialists and historians of the Holocaust, such as Martin Gilbert and David Ceserani, as well as historians of the Jewish diaspora to Britain, including Anthony Grenville and Charmian Brinson. I have read, too, witness testimonies and autobiographies of survivors and exiles. Particularly illuminating in providing the atmosphere of what it was like for refugees living in London in the war is the second volume, *Bombs on Aunt Dainty*, of Judith Kerr's semi-autobiographical trilogy.

Kerr's description of the fear felt by German Jewish refugees in air raid London was one that my mother and her sisters surely shared:

> She [Anna] was lying on the floor with her head under one of the tables, next to Max [her brother] – Mama and Papa were in two chairs on the other side of the [hotel] lounge – and as soon as the room darkened, the thumps and bangs outside became impossible to ignore. She could hear the sound of the planes. A quivering hum like having a mosquito in the room with you only many octaves lower, and every so often the thud of a bomb. The bombs were mostly some distance away, but even so the explosions were quite

loud. Some people, she knew, could tell the difference between German planes and British ones, but they all sounded the same to her. They all sounded German.[6]

I have also gained an enormous amount from fictional accounts located in the era of my parents' youth and early adulthood, such as the noted *The Radetsky March* by Joseph Roth on the last years of the Austro-Hungarian Empire and his elegy to Eastern European Jewry, *The Wandering Jew*, written in Paris in 1936, three years before his death. Such works have suggested *what it must have felt like* to live through periods when everything seemed to be changing – and where seemingly eternal values and familiarities were crumbling away.

Visual media were also hugely informative. For example, I watched a great many films of the 1930s and 1940s, in the hope that they would provide a sense of what it was to be alive at the time. I was particularly interested in how people looked – I found that they were generally smaller and thinner than we are today – and spoke, the accents they had, how they were portrayed, and how the narratives of war and exile were played out. I owe a particular debt to two tremendous television series of the post-war period. The brilliant and heartrending Granada series *The World at War*, first shown in 1973 and directed by Jeremy Isaacs, incorporated previously unseen contemporary footage. Claude Lanzmann's unparalleled *Shoah*, made in 1985, captured vividly the viewpoints of Holocaust survivors, spectators, and perpetrators, as well as the settings of so much horror.

The fact that I started investigating my family history towards the end of my working life, at perhaps a more reflective time, has been advantageous in several ways. First, I have had the time to pursue different threads and storylines. Second, the spread and availability of information and the development of technologies of knowledge distribution (photocopying, Internet communication, digitalisation, mobile phone imaging, and so forth) has made it possible for amateurs and scholars alike to share, scrutinise, and interpret public documents. Access has, thus, been democratised, in the sense that documents are now available to an ever-widening group of people. I have been able to, for example, photocopy the eleven pages of notes on my mother accumulated, largely in the 1940s, by the German Jewish Aid Committee. These are now stored in the archive of the Association of Jewish Refugees (AJR). I've used the National Archive website to access my mother's police file and for a historical background on naturalisation and British citizenship (www.nationalarchive.gov.uk). I've search the Vad Yashem central database of Holocaust victims for confirmation and details of my grandmother's death in Treblinka (www.yadvashem.org) and tracked down my father's brothers and sisters from the Jewish Records Index for Poland (www.jewishgen. org). Email as opposed to 'snail-mail' has likewise been invaluable for seeking out long-lost relatives, scholars, and specialists in similar or related fields of interest and for gaining speedy access to documents and pictures – thus short-circuiting the lengthy investigative process of former times.

One such example, perhaps, is worth mentioning here. After much effort and with the help of a Polish friend, I managed to track down a digital copy of my father's birth certificate, sent to me by the Polish authorities at the cost, incidentally, of one euro. Significantly, it cost a further six euros to expedite the bank transaction. I was looking forward at last to the confirmation of his date and place of birth, which varies considerably in his documentation. However, what arrived was a handwritten document in Russian – perhaps not surprisingly, as Lodz, the place of my father's birth, was part of Russia until 1918. Neither my Polish friend nor I could read Russian. However, I was reminded of a Russian-born former colleague of mine, now living in Florence in Italy. Happily, we were in Facebook contact. I sent her a Facebook message requesting her help. She replied in the affirmative. After confirming her email address, I was able to send her the document as an attachment. Within twenty-four hours of receiving the birth certificate, I had a translation. Such are the joys when friendship and scholarship intersect with digital communication!

However, at other times, progress and the possibility of accessing information has been noticeably slower. The National Archive at

Kew was particularly reluctant to allow the release of information, in particular from my mother's file. My first scrutiny of the file revealed documentation only on my mother's entry into the United Kingdom. Evidently missing was the later documentation on her citizenship applications. On enquiring the reason, I was told that a number of sections had been 'redacted', in other words, removed, due to so-called sensitivity of content. Typically, redaction involves the withholding of pages or whole documents or the blacking out of names or references on released documents. In my mother's case, these redacted parts were designated 'closed' until 2069.

My mother's police record, however, *was* available. And for a small fee, I was able to download it from the National Archives website.

A superficial glance at the cover of her police file reveals important markers in Steffi's refugee life; opened on 10 December 1938, the record shows the date of her actual arrival in Britain two days earlier, her date and place of birth, changes of name (from Dinger to Frocht), and changes of nationality (from German to Austrian).

The information gained from Steffi's police record could not, however, make up for the redactions in her Home Office file. Significantly, I am not alone in facing such difficulties of access. According to Charmian Brinson and Richard Dove's recent book on MI5 surveillance policy, the files of many German and Austrian refugees under surveillance before, during, and after the war remain closed to public scrutiny to this day.[7] The noted Marxist historian and Austrian exile Eric Hobsbawm (1917–2012), for instance, was never allowed access to his security file. On appeal, the whole of my mother's file was eventually released, apart from a few redacted names. However, there was an interesting complexity to the process of revelation.

As we shall see in more detail later, access to my mother's file was granted to me under the terms, not of the recently passed Freedom of Information Act as might be expected, but the Data Protection Act, which gives individuals the right of access to information held on them by government and other public organisations. Since, as her daughter, I was a key figure in my mother's file, it was ruled that I had the right of access to information about *me*. Significantly, my appeal under the Freedom of Information Act failed because disclosure was judged to be against *my* interests, since my mother wanted to keep hidden certain details surrounding my birth. So initially I was not allowed access to the file due to the protection of a living individual – *me*.

The background to these decisions provided another avenue of enquiry. My mother became a target of MI5 surveillance in the first half of the 1950s at the height of the Cold War period when scare stories about the global threat of communism abounded. This is why her file was designated closed for so long. I was curious to know how these security authorities had come into being and, what if anything, was their continuing impact today.

So, of necessity, the boundaries of my investigation expanded dramatically. First set to begin in 1933, when Hitler came to power, and end in 1969, the year of my mother's death, my story now starts with the birth of my maternal grandmother in 1873 and ends with the recent installation in Vienna of 'stolpe' or 'stumbling' stones ('stolpersteine' in German) to commemorate the deaths, at the hands of the Nazis, of my grandmother and great-aunt.

Given its complexity, my account is structured around events, people, and places, as well as chronology. The lives of the three main protagonists of the story are divided into strands that are synchronic and overlapping yet divergent. But first, I convey recent impressions of family places and spaces visited for the purpose of understanding my family history (chapter one) and the account of a wedding in 1963 (chapter two), which provides the setting and context of the book and introduces two of the three main protagonists. Chapter three focuses on the early years of my maternal grandmother, Amalia Dinger, in her home town of Brody. I imagine in this chapter her youth in the shtetl town of Brody, in what is now Ukraine, and in further chapters, her full and exciting life in Vienna (chapter six) as well as her sad end in Treblinka (chapter ten). Chapter four introduces my father, Uszer Frucht, and his early years spent in Poland before he made his journey into exile, first in Belgium (chapter seven) and then in London (chapter nine) and, finally, returning to Belgium, where he remained until his death (chapter eleven). Chapter five similarly explores the childhood and early adulthood in Vienna of my mother, Steffi Dinger, with later chapters focusing on her life in London (chapter eight) and her unsuccessful struggle for British citizenship involving MI6 and Special Branch (chapter twelve). Chapter thirteen seeks to round off the larger story, by recounting the context and impact of a short letter sent by my mother to her future son-in-law again in 1963, just before our marriage. An Afterword entitled 'A Dialogue with the Dead', creates an imaginary dialogue with Amalia, Uszer, and Steffi to envision their responses to the text, their portrayal therein, and what they might think of my contribution as author of their lives.

CHAPTER 1

Places and Spaces

I recently visited Vienna again – I had been before but only as a tourist. In fact, the first time I visited Vienna was when I was about eleven years of age, in the mid-1950s. My mother had arranged the visit with the sister of my Aunt Elsa's late husband Max. Tilda Mauruber lived in Vienna and, I later learnt, was a concentration camp survivor. I was to spend two weeks on an exchange visit with a Viennese girl of similar age, Heide, the daughter of a local doctor. Heide was then to stay with me in London in the following year. There are a number of things that stand out in my memory from that first Viennese visit. I gained no sense that Vienna had been recently reduced by rubble in the war and, indeed, do not recall noticing any bomb damage. What most impressed me was the prosperity and glamour of Vienna at the time, compared to the greyness of bomb-damaged London. I noted that Heide's house was more opulent than those I was most familiar with at home, but I put this down to the fact that her father was a doctor. A second memory was the agony of mosquito bites following an evening dinner outside, on the banks of the Danube, and desperately trying not to scratch my arms and legs through the hot and, for me, sleepless Viennese night. A better memory was being the only one of Heide's friends one afternoon at an outdoor tea dance to be asked to take the floor by a dark handsome stranger.

By far the most vivid memories of this period in Vienna were the heated arguments I had with Heide and her family on the impact of wartime events on our two countries and, in particular, curiously, whether Hitler might be described as a great man. Presumably, the family knew that I was Jewish, so in retrospect, arguing from this position seems tactless to say the very least. I remember being deeply shocked because I had learnt that the Nazis had wreaked havoc in Vienna as well as across the world and because the war was relatively recent. Heide and her father tried to convince me that 'greatness' was to do with historical visibility and impact, rather than ethical standing, and seemed impervious to what such an argument might mean to the daughter of a Viennese Jewish refugee. I was horrified and argued passionately against Hitler's so-called 'greatness', but these arguments left me with a bitter taste about what I now recognise as the complicity of many Austrians in Hitler's rise to power.

The holiday arrangement was adhered to, and Heide stayed with us in London for a couple of weeks the following summer. But following that, not surprisingly, communications between the two families ceased.

On a more recent visit, some four decades later, I was more purposeful. I was in Vienna to find out about my mother's family, where they lived, and what happened to them. My mother was always nostalgic about the city of her birth – where she'd lived out her childhood and which had been the centre of her youthful hopes and later fears. But again on this later visit, I did not like Vienna very much. For all the grandeur of its majestic buildings and its positioning at the heart of Europe, it seemed to me to be a city without compassion. It was certainly, for a long time, a city in denial about its historical legacy and its harsh treatment in the Nazi era of those who opposed the regime or were singled out for extinction.

I saw on this visit that, like all cities, Vienna has several distinctive parts. There is the inner part that has been made attractive for the tourists, full of massive imperial buildings that provide the showcasing of official Vienna – formal state buildings, imposing museums, the ancient university, the grand opera house, and the lively arts and theatre districts. All of this reflects Vienna's historical high point as the capital of the great Austro-Hungarian Empire. This part of Vienna also presumably provides a sense of historical identity for present-day Viennese. The outer part of the city is where most Viennese live seemingly prosperous and happy lives in modern well-appointed post-war apartments, from which they commute to their jobs in the centre via the modern and efficient bus and metro systems.

However, there are parts of the city between the inner and outer, where the 'others' live. These others are incomers from other European countries and migrants of various hues from different parts of the world. Included in this 'other' group are the seven thousand or so Jews who have made Vienna their home, despite (or because of) the fates of their grandparents' generation and of those farther back. These are mainly Jews from Russia and Eastern Europe, economic migrants rather than refugees from overt persecution or threats to their lives. When visiting the areas in which they now live, areas that were historically Jewish areas, there is a noticeable discreteness about the Jewish presence that is painful to see. One catches fleeting glimpses here and there of young bearded men leaving their daughters at school in a courtyard behind a fence or of older similarly bearded men pulling on cigarettes as they scurry across the square near the heavily guarded central city synagogue. There are few visible cultural celebrations of Jewish life as it is lived today, although there are many reminders of what it used to be. As Lydia, our guide to 'Jewish Vienna' says, there is little to be seen *inside* of the old Jewish Vienna. Mostly, all we can see are outdoor memorials to the dead; wall plaques and *stolpe* stones (plaques inserted into the cobbles) celebrate and mourn the lives of loved ones and relatives who otherwise would be just numbers in a catalogue of Jewish humanity murdered between 1933 and 1945. I promise myself that I will lay stones in commemoration of my grandmother, Amalia, and her sister, Frieda, at the place from which they were deported.

For those like me seeking to know about the history of their Viennese families, however, there is no open-armed welcome, no sense of *mea culpa*. Rather, the middle-aged Viennese citizens we come across seem irritated by our presence and our questions, which perhaps disrupt their collective memories of the past or wishes for the future. We are welcomed by the institutions and bodies that have been created to help us find out about *our* past, for example, where our forebears lived and what happened to them after 1938 when the systematic process of discrimination, deportation, and murder began. But I also gain the impression that this wretched part of Vienna's history is strictly kosher[8], in other words, for Jews only and definitely not for the consumption of the wider public. This reticence on the part of the Viennese fails, however, to halt my questioning. Rather, it makes me all the more persistent in seeking out the inevitable and horrible truth. It is in an out-of-the-way district of Vienna, across the Danube Canal, that one part of my story starts, that of my grandmother and mother. I later find out much information about their family and the city they loved, although mainly from specifically Jewish organisations and archives.

Yet, I had two parents, though they were rarely in the same place at the same time. My father was also Jewish. But he was from Lodz in Poland, and I knew less about his family for reasons that will become apparent as my story unfolds. My father lost eighty members of his extended family, including brothers and sisters and their families, at the hands of the Nazis. I still cannot imagine how he and others like him were able to live with that loss.

So Lodz too was on my itinerary in the search for my family. Compared to Vienna, the city is run-down and neglected. The main street, Ulica Piotrkowska, is reputedly the longest main thoroughfare in Europe. About three kilometres in length, it edges towards the centre of town, lined by mostly well-preserved, early twentieth-century art nouveau house fronts. The Hotel Grand – an intricately decorated *jugendstil* building, with many of its original features intact – is particularly impressive. Outside, etched into the pavement, are the names of film artists and directors who stayed at the hotel a long, long time ago.

Lodz is a much less visibly proud city than Vienna. It has neither Vienna's glamour nor its pretensions. Its history was predominantly industrial, and though it was never a country's capital, its Jews faced the same tragic outcome as did the Jews of Vienna and Warsaw, Poland's present-day capital. Only two survived of the eight hundred thousand or so Lodz Jews who passed through the local death camp, Chelmno.

Despite Poland's anti-Semitic reputation, I sense less antagonism towards my search for information here than I found in Vienna. Nevertheless, as in Vienna, little remains of the pre-war Jewish presence. An exception is a massive Jewish cemetery, apparently the largest of its kind in Europe, which includes an uncultivated field dedicated to the people who died in the ghetto. I find myself moved by its size and its wildness and by the stone tablets commemorating the deaths of Jewish families, some in English, on the walls of the cemetery. Again, I determine to put one such tablet up for my father's family, if and when I find out more about them.

The cemetery is far too big for me even to consider looking for family members, so I am advised to contact the Jewish Community Centre nearby. The archivist there is helpful but cool. I am provided with names that may have links to my father's family. This leads later to important information and documentation, particularly concerning his parents, and his brothers and sisters.

Lodz's Poznański Palace, built in the second half of the nineteenth century by Izrael Poznański, the son of a thread and ribbon seller who became a wealthy Jewish textile industrialist, alongside his factory complex (now a retail park), provides another indication of a previous Jewish presence. It evokes the lifestyle of bourgeois Jews in Lodz, long gone. The palace is now a museum dedicated to Jewish artists who came from or were somehow associated with the city. It includes the works and artefacts of the pianist Arthur Rubinstein, composer Alexander Tansman, poet Julian Tuwim, writer Jerzy Kosinski, and Holocaust diplomat Jan Karski, all displayed against the original richly ornate art nouveau design of interiors and furniture.

Then, as a contrast, there is the train journey, with Anna a Polish-speaking friend, to Brody. There, in what is now Western Ukraine, my maternal grandmother's family lived before the turn of the twentieth century. Previously a predominantly Jewish town, Brody went into sharp decline in the 1920s and 1930s when many of its Jewish inhabitants left for the New World. Those who remained were murdered by the Nazis when the ghetto was 'cleared' in 1942. Few returned after 1945, and now there are none. The train from Lvov, the capital of the region, to Brody is a local one, stopping at every small place along the way. Sometimes a horse and cart await the collection of a passenger. Vendors on the train sell everything from newspapers to sweets to household goods. There are beggars too. The journey takes two hours, and we eventually draw into an unexpectedly modern-looking station, again with an art nouveau interior and candelabra.

The early sunshine has disappeared by now, and we have only a few hours in Brody before we are due to catch the train back. We take a taxi to the Jewish cemetery, which is mentioned in one of the guidebooks as worth seeing. Again, the hope is that I might recognise a family name. Under darkening clouds, we come to an enclosed field full of mottled and pockmarked gravestones, all pointing in one direction. Out of the ragged waving grass, rectangular headstones loom high, each covered in indecipherable (to us) Hebrew script. It is eerie and unnerving, and I am pleased that there is someone with me. A particular Stanley Spencer painting comes to mind – of graves opening and the dead awakening. We quickly move on.

Brody, with its potholed roads, neglected buildings, and little evidence of modern life, does not impress. The taxi takes us to the derelict synagogue, sturdy still despite having been laid waste by the

Nazis. Why the ruin has been allowed to remain we do not know. We guess that the area surrounding the synagogue was once a Jewish enclave, but there is little evidence of a Jewish presence now, and the buildings are all of post-war origin and design.

By chance, we find a cafe hidden behind a door in a block of shops and step into another world. Here, groups of people lunch at long tables or, one assumes for privacy, in curtained booths. All kinds of Ukrainian and Polish delicacies are on show. We order fish, potatoes, beetroots, and tomatoes, washed down by beer and tea. Other diners, men and women, are knocking back small shots of vodka, though it is only early afternoon. It proves to be a wonderfully exotic experience, but indicative perhaps that any fragments of Jewish culture that existed before have long gone.

I have visited other family places as part of my investigation. Among these is Brussels, where I learnt about my father and met his 'other' family. I had become aware of their existence when my father paid a visit to London after the death of my mother but knew little more. By means of the online Brussel's telephone directory, I managed to find the address of a half-sister, Augustine, and then another half-sister, Clara, and then their children. Problems arose, however, from the fact that the various generations – belonging to the Brussels' family and my own – are not only chronologically but culturally discontinuous. I was my father's youngest child by fourteen years, so I am a decade and a half younger than my half-sisters; their children are only a decade or so younger than me, and my children are only a decade younger than their half-cousins. So I was addressed as 'auntie' by Claude, who is only a few years younger than me, which I found, perhaps unreasonably, patronising. I made two visits to see my new family in Brussels – the first to find out more about my father and his other family and the second to accompany my children on a visit to see members of their hitherto unknown extended family.

Initially, we received a warm welcome, and there was much curiosity on both sides. We saw family resemblances everywhere, and on first meeting my younger half-sister, Augustine, I had a premonition of what I might look like in fifteen years' time. But it turned out that history and environment and nurture rather than nature matter more than family and blood. While, for two or three days, we were able to socialise and talk about ourselves and our families, we found that we were divided by work, politics, and place. The Brussels family is predominantly 'in business', the diamond trade included; mine are mostly educational professionals of one sort or other. The Brussels' family is vehemently pro-Israel, and we were not. They are anti-immigrant, and we are not. They regularly attend the synagogue, and we do not. They have married 'in', and we have not. In the end, this caused a schism that appeared unbridgeable. Moreover, they appeared uncomfortable with the notion that their father and grandfather had another family elsewhere and expressed interest neither in his London 'wife' nor in the investigation that had led me to them. I presented them with a digital copy of Uszer's Brussels file but was not convinced that they would ever look at it. What they had to say about Uszer, my and their father and grandfather, was, in fact, quite scathing – they spoke of his unrepentant communism, his poor record in providing for his family, his bad driving, and so on. A half-niece (daughter of Uszer's oldest child, Henri, now deceased) who I found later via Facebook did, however, profess a greater degree of affection and respect for her paternal grandfather. This perhaps suggests an alternative family story waiting to be told.

Apart from one cousin in the United Kingdom, Alec Spencer, the son of my mother's youngest sister, Trude, my only two remaining cousins on my mother's side live in the United States. George Bertish, the son of my mother's sister Tilda, now lives in Florida. His younger sister Frieda Ziering née Bertish (and her husband and children) lived in Newark, New Jersey, for a long time but have recently moved to Arizona. We shall see in more detail later how George, who was born in Vienna in 1936, escaped with his mother, heading eastwards across Russia to the United States of America in 1942. After completing school and university (the first member of the extended family to go to university), he made a career in the army. Following a painful divorce, he later became an evangelical Baptist and Republican Party supporter. We, my cousin Alec and I, have retained only occasional contact with him since his mother died in 2001. Frieda, named after the great-aunt who died in the Lodz Ghetto, was born after the war in the United States and has chosen to keep her Jewish identity and her family's traditionally liberal politics.

We visited our American cousins, Alec and I, in May 2008. The meeting was difficult to arrange, as they lived a long way away from each other and seemed rarely to be in contact. We arranged our trip to Newark around the fact that George was attending a college reunion at Rutgers University nearby; so we were able to spend a couple of days with them together and apart. Again, what was striking is the huge role that environment has played in the lives of we four first cousins, the children of three sisters from Vienna. Only Frieda, a college-educated administrator by occupation, could be said to be a practising Jew. Alec, living in Dollar in Scotland, identifies primarily as a humanist but acknowledges his Jewish background. George, who served twenty-three years on active military duty in the US army, has renounced Judaism altogether. After a stint in Vietnam and having accumulated many awards and medals for bravery, he retired with the rank of lieutenant colonel. Somewhere along the way, he became a gun-toting, God-fearing Baptist. I identify as Jewish culturally and historically but am, I suppose, an atheist.

Despite George's possibly ironic evaluation of Alec and me as 'pinko', wishy-washy liberals, he was happy to provide an account of his escape with his mother from war-torn Europe, though it was from the memory and perspective of the six year-old he was at the time. Once again, neither Frieda nor George expressed much interest in the investigation that had led us to them. Nor were they interested in their parents' past. They were quick to excuse themselves on the grounds of the death of their father, Max, long before he could tell them what had happened and the reluctance of their mother to speak about 'that time'.

So it is clear that spaces and places have an important significance, both for the stories that make up the rest of this book and for the context in which the book was written. I find it difficult to understand why so many members of my extended family in other countries have so little interest in their own history. Perhaps that history could explain why they have taken that position and become the people they are. I consider, for example, the Belgian family's pro-Israel, conservative, and angry stance or George, a clever and ambitious man, who did his best to leave his Jewish and 'foreign' past behind him on arriving in America. And I suppose my history – growing up in a progressive and tolerant though secretive environment – has led me to be the person I am, in particular, concerning my curiosity about and imagining of the past.

CHAPTER 2

The Wedding, 1963

I begin this chapter with a wedding photograph because it is said that photographs do not lie – although this one comes pretty close to doing just that. The photograph, secured in a well-thumbed wedding photo album with a white leatherette cover, popular in decades past, is familiar to me. It is one of fifteen or so others selected to commemorate the occasion.

I have chosen this picture to start a story that will spread in different ways across this book. It portrays two of the book's main protagonists, Steffi and Uszer Frocht (or so they are named in the wedding invitations), as well as the person who connected them, their daughter Gaby (me). What message does this photograph transmit?

What can it tell us? First, the picture is a relatively conventional wedding photo, carefully posed, perhaps old-fashioned to modern-day eyes. There is the bride looking quite radiant. Perhaps she is twenty or so or a few years older. Her dress is the usual, traditional white, perhaps a little on the plain side for today's taste. But she looks as happy as a bride should on her wedding day, the so-called best day of her life. I am biased, though, because she is, or rather was, me. The bride's parents look happy too – prosperous, dressed-up, all-of-a-piece. They seem unruffled and calm, smiling, perhaps a little on the old side to be parents. Could they be the bride's grandparents? But usually grandparents do not get the bride all to themselves in such a wedding picture. So, yes, they are her parents. The father is in formal dress with bow tie, no doubt hired for the day, and in some of the photographs, he is wearing a top hat. People observed at the time that he bore a striking resemblance to Billy Cotton, a popular bandleader in the 1950s. The mother's hat has been especially bought for the occasion, and she is wearing a formal dress and matching jacket in a silky fabric, home-made but not at all amateurish.

Note the picture is black and white. This must, therefore, be a time when monochrome photo portraits for big family occasions were still common. This is a special occasion without a doubt, but it can be assumed that it has been organised on a tight budget. The bride's headband and backcombed hair have the look of the 1960s about them; in fact, it is 1963. The bride is eighteen, going on nineteen. Her mother is sixty and her father, a couple of years older than that. At the time, the bride thinks her father is sixty-one (born 20 September 1901). However, most of his documents, which she has not yet seen, put his birth date at 1900, a year earlier; one document indicates that he might be as old as sixty-five. The bride's parents are old enough to be her grandparents, but they are in fact her *parents*. It may be assumed, then, that she is the offspring of a late liaison or dalliance or perhaps a second marriage.

What else does the picture reveal? Where was it taken? Where do these people come from? One thing not perhaps immediately apparent is that the picture was taken in the bride's front room in

North London. Now, we know that London and other big cities are places where migrants and lost souls congregate. It is probable that the threesome originate not from Britain, but from elsewhere? If so, from where? Put another way, if the bride is eighteen and it is 1963, she was born around 1944, towards the end of the Second World War. You might then calculate that her parents may have met during wartime, perhaps while working for the war effort or because they were escaping from something or someone. Given the background to the war, it is likely that the older people in the photograph may have escaped from Nazism and/or persecution of the Jews. 'Oh no!' Here comes the sigh. 'Not another story about persecuted and suffering Jews.'

I hope that the story that will unfold is not just another typical story of Jewish suffering and oppression; yet I have to admit that the main figures in the photograph *are* (or were) Jews, and elements in the story might be familiar. The most important thing about this picture is not that the participants are Jewish. Nor is it that that the photograph shows something we recognise as familiar – a conventional wedding grouping (albeit one that clearly took place sometime in the past). The most important thing is that the picture is based on a lie, in fact, many lies. It is a lie both in the way the individuals are positioned in the photograph and in the sense that many of the people at the wedding are themselves involved in maintaining the lie. The bride in the centre is the most unknowing. She thinks she 'knows' that beside her are her parents, who both love her and wish her well, though she is also aware that they have not lived together except for several years around her birth. She knows that the wedding has been arranged to make her small family look normal and respectable – respectability is a precious asset and commodity in the 1960s. Being also a child of the sixties, she is in the process of rejecting what seem to be the stifling rules of the older generation and so has not been particularly interested or involved in the formal organisation of the wedding; she has left all that to her mother.

The story the bride has been told is that her parents met and fell in love during wartime. They were married, but through force of circumstance, were compelled to live apart for much of her and their lives. Indeed, at the time the picture was taken, they had been living for many years in different countries, her mother in London and her father in Brussels. She had seen her father on a number of fleeting occasions but lived with and was brought up by her mother and her two aunts and their families.

The bride's mother, however, harbours a different set of perceptions and memories about her past. She has been careful about the explanations she has given to her daughter about why they are not part of a conventional family. In particular, she has sought to protect her daughter from stigma by deliberately withholding important information, which has a bearing on the form of wedding that is taking place. That the marriage has been conducted in a liberal rather than orthodox synagogue and the fact that all three in the picture share the same family name – Frocht – would not be a surprise to most people. Regarding the first, these are modern times, and it is increasingly acceptable that the marriage is taking place in a progressive rather than a more orthodox religious setting. In the case of the second, parents and their children almost invariably share the same name. However, a great deal of effort has gone in to ensuring that these conventional elements of a wedding are in place. In fact, because of the bride's unconventional parental arrangements, she has been denied the possibility of marrying in an orthodox (mainstream) synagogue. She does not know that this is why the marriage is taking place elsewhere; only her mother and certain friends and relatives know and understand why she has been judged not good enough for orthodox Jewry. Ensuring that all three are seen to share the same family name, so important for the printed invitations (see below) has taken a much, much longer time.

The bride's father also holds secrets close to himself, and although bluff and cheery in the photographs, speaks half-truths and sets out to deceive. He has seemingly appeared from nowhere, looking plump and respectable (that word again) though he has been long denied legal entry into Britain. Nonetheless, he has managed to make at least one day-long visit annually to see his London 'family' and has even been able, on this occasion, to extend his visit to a couple of days in order to attend. His 'occasional' wife (Steffi) always seems pleased to see him when he appears and indeed becomes noticeably skittishly girlish; less so his British-born daughter, who dislikes the smell of him (of Gauloise cigarettes and cigar smoke) and having to touch the stunted thumb on his nicotine-stained left hand.

The older wedding guests retain memories of wartime relationships torn asunder by the passing years and no doubt appreciate why the cover-up is necessary. They take care not to give anything away and even seem to be enjoying themselves. Perhaps they are relieved, like the bride's mother, that a potential disaster has been transformed into a triumph. The bride has had a somewhat wayward and unruly adolescence, so there is a sense of relief that she is 'settling down'. The bridegroom too has been inducted into the family story, which implicates his bride, and of which she is ignorant; but he has been sworn to secrecy. Later, much, much later, he will admit to his then ex-wife that the secret he promised to conceal, though perhaps important to her, was then and would remain unimportant to him – it would be swiftly forgotten in the busy family-building period of the couple's younger married life. Only the bride and perhaps some of her close friends attending the wedding remain ignorant. What a fool she (and perhaps they) feel when eventually the truth comes out!

It all starts so well. Gaby and Philip want to get married for the usual reasons (intimacy, sex, adventure, independence). In these times, in the early 1960s, there is not much money around, particularly for immigrant and working-class families. The so-called swinging sixties have not yet got going, money is tight, and families are scrunched together in small living spaces. Young people seek to break out in different ways, one of which is marriage. Marriage was more popular then than it is now. Young women like Gaby of immigrant background, who struggle for their identity in a confusing and frequently humbling world, find that acquiring a boyfriend, a husband, and later children provides an initial solution to entry into the world of which they are part but where they also often seem to be outsiders. For the moment anyway, at the time of her marriage and immediately afterwards, Gaby is able to achieve an identity of acceptability and respectability – those qualities to which her mother aspires but finds so difficult to acquire.

Weddings then were not the big occasions they are today. The more status-conscious parents of the time often opened a wedding fund on the birth of their daughters so as to be able to give them a good 'send-off' when the time came. This is the case with the bride's Aunt Fanny and Uncle Joe, who, despite lack of wealth, are able to arrange 'fairy-tale' weddings for their two daughters, Mali and Dena. These were exceptional affairs for the time, highlights of Gaby's childhood. In particular, she recalls the wedding breakfasts, which took place in seemingly grand hotels and included five or six courses of rich exotic food, and, joy of joys, dancing.

Gaby remembers partnering her mother who, like many middle-aged women of the time, possessed a wonderfully comfortable shelf-like bosom and round tummy, and she fondly recalls the feeling of bouncing off both as she waltzed around the room. She remembers well the dresses she wore for both weddings – a blue-flowered empire dress for the first and a wonderful, apricot-coloured fitted dress with a wide white collar for the second. Both were handmade by Steffi.

There is a reason for telling this story about weddings and dresses. The wedding in the photo takes the form it does because the bride's mother is anxious to impress her cousin Fanny, to whom she is close but of whom she is more than a little afraid. She owes an immeasurable debt of gratitude to Fanny, who is responsible for her survival and that of her two sisters and, ultimately, for her present relatively comfortable life. Fanny is a first cousin, the daughter of Steffi's uncle on his mother's side. This uncle came to London in the early part of the twentieth century from Brody, and for many years, he owned a shoe shop in London's East End. Shoe shops seem to run in the family, as Steffi's parents also managed a shoe shop in Vienna. Anyhow, Fanny, who is a couple of years older than Steffi, was an office worker before her marriage, which was unusual for a Jewish East End working-class girl in the 1920s. Her subsequent earnings enabled her to afford to visit the Viennese side of the family in 1927.

As the photograph suggests, Steffi and Fanny hit it off from the first. A decade on when the Nazis invaded Austria and panic set it, Fanny did everything she could to help her Steffi and her other cousins escape. She stood as guarantor of employment so that they could enter Britain legitimately as refugees. This was a huge risk for Fanny on two counts. First, as the rest of the English part of the family reminded her at the time, were the Nazis to invade, the presence of German nationals (Austria was then part of the greater Germany) would imperil not only Fanny's immediate family but them also. Fanny was regretful until the day she died about the stance taken by her sisters and brothers and their failure to come to the rescue of other members of the Viennese side of the family. Second, in guaranteeing to take in Steffi and her two sisters, Fanny, a married working-class woman with two small daughters, laid herself open to accusations of perjury. She promised that she would provide jobs (and payment) for her Austrian cousins so that they would not be a financial burden on the British state. Due to Fanny's bravery and, we might say, chutzpah, not only were Steffi and her two sisters allowed into Britain, but they also had a roof over their heads through the worst years of the Blitz – until their English improved, they could get work, and they could afford to rent a place of their own.

So perhaps the reason the wedding is particularly significant for Steffi, Fanny, and the older people present is becoming clear. For the bride and groom, his relatives, and their friends, it is an important day without doubt, but for the usual reasons. For the young couple, it means the beginning of freedom and independence and a new phase in their lives. For some of the guests, it presents a rare opportunity to dress up and have a party. For the bride's mother, her father, and the rest, though, it means much more.

For them, this occasion is more than just the binding of two young people together in marriage or the fusing of two families. It is also about showing what has been achieved since their arrival in their new country, both to their fellow immigrants and to locally born relatives, in-laws, neighbours, and friends. It is about displaying the extent to which they, as immigrants, have kept faith with the traditions and expectations of the old country – and also how well they have responded to the new. The 1963 wedding thus demonstrates certain things; that, for example, despite what has gone before and all the traumas and uncertainties of the past, the bride's mother (with or without spouse) is able to do right by her daughter. She shows that she is able to put on a proper 'English' wedding, albeit a modest one, and accomplish a legitimate marriage according to Jewish custom. Also that the formal conventions – such as ensuring the appropriately attired presence of the main actors – have been adhered to. Decencies have been preserved so that the past does not encroach too much on the present.

This has been achieved only with careful prudence and planning. Steffi knows, for example, that her daughter, unlike many present-day brides, is not interested in the process and pageant of getting married. She and her husband-to-be just want 'to do it' and be free of the authority and influence of their parents and the older generation. So Steffi is able to go ahead and negotiate with the synagogue and prepare the formalities. She personally stitches the bridesmaids' dresses and arranges for a dressmaker friend to do the same for the bride's ensemble. Finances allow only for a modest wedding breakfast for a small number of guests (thirty-five or so) in the front room at home. Yet Steffi is able to observe certain niceties; she engages kosher[9] caterers, hires a waitress for the day, and orders extra chairs and tables for the sit-down meal – coming to the rather modest cost of £63 plus £10 deposit.

The invitation list includes the parents of the bride and groom, of course, plus three small bridesmaids, the bridegroom's brother and sister and their families, and several aunts and uncles on the bridegroom's side. On the bride's side, there is Trude (Steffi's youngest sister); her husband, John; and their only child Alec. Steffi's other sister is missing, as she has died suddenly some nine months earlier. Sadly, Trude has not long to live either, only several more years, although she is the youngest by far of the sisters. Other guests on the bride's side include the aforementioned Fanny and her husband, Joe; their granddaughter, who is one of the bridesmaids; plus one of Fanny's sisters, Sally, who is also close to Steffi. Present also are Leo, the London-based brother-in-law of Steffi's sister Tilda in the United States, and his non-Jewish Austrian wife, also named Steffi. And rounding out the guests is the bride's mother's closest friend, the diminutive Mina Klein.

In addition to relatives on the groom's side, the wedding party is completed by the bridal pair's friends and neighbours, although few of them are visible in the group picture above. The bride and groom are both active in local youth politics, as are Trude and John, both local Labour Party councillors. One of their neighbours on the wedding list is the current local mayor. So, the wedding is profiled in the local paper – much to Steffi's delight.

The relationships between wedding guests are perhaps more difficult to gauge because of the complexity and distinctiveness of various familial and friendship connections, particularly as they involve people who have been torn from loved families and places. But the significant thing is that, apart from the bridegroom, it is only the relatives and older generation of friends on the bride's side who know or suspect the extent of the effort that has been expended to make this event so ordinary and un-newsworthy.

But what is the secret that Steffi has striven so hard to keep from her daughter? You have no doubt guessed. It is that the brides' parents are not married, and therefore, the bride is illegitimate. Indeed, her father has a thriving 'first' family in Brussels, which is equally ignorant of the existence of another family in London. The outline of what happened will be detailed later as the story unfolds, but a brief summary will suffice here.

Steffi and Uszer met at a social event for Austrian refugees in 1942. Uszer was a sometime actor in an amateur Yiddish theatrical group, and Steffi was secretary at the Jewish refugee social centre where he was performing. Both alone in a strange country in wartime and fearing that the worst had happened to their relatives and loved ones, they were drawn together, moved in together, and had a child. At the end of the war, Uszer found his first family – a wife and three children – had survived, although evidently, none were in good health. He outstayed the period of his visa when he visited them, and because he'd initially entered the country illegally, the British authorities refused to allow him back into Britain, and so that was that.

The story of their meeting was, of course, much more complicated than that, as we shall see later. As already noted, the story covers the first half of the twentieth century, though it originates in the nineteenth century, and also spills over into the second part of the twentieth century down to the present day. It starts in Eastern Europe, in the Austro-Hungarian Empire and on the Russian and Polish borders. It moves westwards, ending finally in Britain and also in Belgium, though its roots trail across the Atlantic. It involves the Jewish pogroms of Eastern Europe, the promises of Soviet-style communism to the dispossessed, the devastatingly long reach of fascism, tales of persecution and escape and of resettlement, and further disorder in the Cold War era. Finally, it comes to some kind of resolution and reconciliation in new times and new places.

It is a difficult tale to tell because it lacks boundaries, continually stretching outwards and inwards. Its various narratives are both familiar and strange. It is also a constructed story, as most stories are, in the sense that there are many gaps and unknowns that require imaginative leaps of faith and understanding. To untangle the various elements of the story and its context, I have sought to ground it in the narratives of three individuals. This approach allows me to provide context and background as individual lives are played out but also results in the occasional retelling of themes and events, perhaps from a different perspective, with the aim, not of repetition, but of reflection and affirmation.

CHAPTER 3

Amalia in Brody, 1873–1899

Here, I show where the family story starts, or rather one particular part. I also explore now and later on why particular events that make up what is now called the Holocaust will forever be the most important historical events for Jewish people, wherever and whenever they live. It might be said that we have heard or read similar stories and that what I write will say nothing new. Yet for me, it is important to go through it all again. I hope that, in the telling of their stories, my grandmother Amalia and other members of my family are lifted out of and extracted from the unnamed millions who perished at the terrible time when the entire world seemed to be at war – and identified.

I never knew my maternal grandmother, who until recently was just a faded sepia image in an old photograph, a name on a list, the subject of an official message of condolence. My mother did not talk about her own mother, perhaps because it was too painful. Thus, I have had only fleeting glimpses into Amalia's life.

I have tried to imagine her as the person my mother loved best (apart perhaps from me) and who most shaped her character and perspective on life, which in turn helped shape what I have become. In trying to put together her story, I see her life in three parts – first, her childhood in a small rural shtetl town; second, her busy life in a cosmopolitan Vienna in her early married life and middle years, and third, the short, terrible end to her life. Her husband, David Hirsch Dinger, my maternal grandfather, died in 1928, and she became head of household. It is these earlier parts of her life that I wish to revive and not just the later, darker third part. So to start with, I explore the hopes and expectation of her childhood spent in the small Jewish town of Brody.

Amalia (also known as Malke, her Jewish name) Moszkowicz Dinger was born on 4 November 1873 in Brody in the far eastern part of the Austro-Hungarian Empire. She was a member of the Moszkowicz-Dinger family, part of the deeply religious Jewish community and culture of a shtetl town. Brody, as I have seen, is now a very different from the town in which Amalia was born and grew up.

Like many places in this story, Brody has a long history. It lies in the middle of a great plain, which archaeological excavations have identified as a site of human habitation long before the name Brody appeared formally. The original name Brod means ford and was derived from the town's proximity to the Styr River where the river narrows and could, therefore, be forded and crossed. Brody lies in the western part of Ukraine close to the present Polish border. It is over fifty miles from the largest city in the region, L'viv (also known as L'vov and in German as Lemberg), where a brother of Amalia's, Sigmund, lived in 1899. It also lies 187 miles west of Kiev, Ukraine's present-day capital, and only a few miles from the previous border with Imperial Russia. Due to its proximity to Russia, Brody had many conquerors over the centuries and was governed by many regimes and empires, yet it also thrived on the trade (of goods and ideas) that this location brought.

The modern town began as a military outpost, established by a Polish military leader Stanislaw Koniecpolski, who built fortifications in 1633 to repel the invading Tartars and their Turkish allies. The town remained under the control of Polish overlords, though it attracted significant numbers of Armenians, Greeks, Jews, and even Scots when laws were passed allowing more autonomy to Polish cities and villages. By the end of the seventeenth century, four hundred Jewish families were living in Brody, the prosperity of which may be judged by the construction of a large synagogue, generally referred to as the 'old fortress synagogue'. Built to withstand assaults, the synagogue was a sturdy cube with fortifications at its base and still exists today, though in ruined form.

Following the destruction of the Jewish quarter of Brody by fire in 1696, Jews were granted permission to live in other areas of the city and to expand their range of trades to include distilling spirits, making and selling handicrafts, and conducting other commercial enterprises in return for payment of higher taxes. By mid-eighteenth century, Jews dominated trade in Brody, and the town's Jewish artisans were famous for weaving and metalwork. But safety had to be bought. For example, during a four-year war that led to the partition of Poland in 1772 and the formation of the region of Galicia, the Jews of Brody were made responsible for ensuring that armies passing through the city were properly fed. Following this war, Brody, along with the rest of Galicia, came under Austrian jurisdiction, one outcome of which was reduction in the tax burden on Jewish merchants. Another was greater freedom for Jewish craftsmen and their guilds.

Brody's prestige was enhanced in 1779 when it was made a free trade city, a status it enjoyed for more than a century, with the Napoleonic wars and various trade blockades elsewhere further enhancing its reputation as a major conduit city or channel of trade between Russia and the Austro-Hungarian Empire. Brody thus extended its economic influence way beyond Poland and Austria to become one of the most important trading centres of Central and Eastern Europe of the time.

By the 1790s, the Jewish citizens of Brody were trading hemp, linen, wax, honey, and tobacco in exchange for cotton, French silk, spices, beads, jewels, sugar, wool, feathers, horses, and fur. The town expanded as new houses were built. Brody's prosperity reached its peak of influence in the early to middle part of the nineteenth century. Besides its commercial importance, the city was of great Talmudic and scholarly importance, in which different Jewish orthodox groups such as the Talmudists and Hasidim could argue and coexist.

By Amalia's birth in 1873, however, Brody had begun its slow economic decline. Initially due to the re-imposition of trade restrictions by the Viennese-based government and, later, to the cancellation of the free trade patent, the decline continued into the new century. This decline was exacerbated by the lack of industry to offset the downturn in trade. Industry and the work opportunities which it promised, were more of a magnet to other urban areas at the time.

Without work, attracted to the sophisticated urbanism of Vienna, and wishing to escape both the religious shackles of Jewish shtetl life and religious persecution, young couples like Amalia and David made plans to move westwards to Vienna. Others, like a sister of David's, left for England, and yet others embarked on the long journey to America. Between 1880 and 1910, the Jewish population of Brody halved. Brody came under Polish control once more in 1918 at the end of the First World War. Interwar Polish society was less hostile to Jewish citizens than that in other European countries. The Jewish community in Brody continued to survive and develop, even if many of its younger people saw their future elsewhere. Pre-war Brody is remembered with affection by Boleslaw Kulczycki, whose father took part in the liberation from the Nazis, of Lublin, Warsaw, and Berlin.[10] He recalled:

> Beautiful Roman and Greek-Orthodox churches and synagogues graced the town, and old cemeteries chronicled the history of Brody's inhabitants. On a Sunday, people would walk along lovely main streets, such as Gold and Mickiewicza or relax in a park in the center of town, called Rojekowka, which was close to my family's home. Young boys admired the soldiers marching on parade to the accompaniment of a brass band, and the cavalry soldiers proudly riding astride beautifully groomed horses. These soldiers were our heroes. Youngsters paraded in boy scout uniforms...
> It was a time of happiness and tranquillity.

However, by 1939, Soviet airplanes were bombing the town and a Soviet regime was speedily imposed, alongside the deportation Brody's wealthiest citizens. People went hungry, and 'enemies of the people' were taken to the nearby forest and shot. 'The atmosphere in the town was gloomy.' However, the situation worsened dramatically with the departure of the Soviet soldiers and the appearance of the Germans in 1942. Brody's Jewish inhabitants were first crowded into a ghetto and later deported and murdered, mainly at Auschwitz. The Nazi era signalled the end of Jewish shtetl life. Of the 13,000 Jews living in Brody prior to the outbreak of the war, only 88 people survived, and even fewer returned.

By this time, however, Amalia and her husband and, I assume, other members of the family were long gone, although some may have remained in Brody until the end. There is no way of knowing, as Holocaust victims were not dignified with graves; Jewish burials had more or less ceased by 1938.

Interestingly, despite the huge loss of Jews in the Nazi era and beyond, Ukrainian Jews remain the fourth largest Jewish community in the world (after those in the United States, Israel, and France). They are mainly concentrated in the capital, Kiev (110,000), Dniepropetrovsk (60,000), Kharkov (45,000), and Odessa (45,000). The latter is where the Dinger family may have originated, though members were also scattered among many of the smaller towns. However, in Western Ukraine (former Galicia), only a small remnant of the former large Jewish population remains – approximately 12,000, divided between L'viv and Chernivtsi. None are in Brody. Nowadays, it is only a few older Jewish people who claim Yiddish as their mother tongue (in 1926, it was over three-quarters) with the majority of present-day Ukrainian Jews speaking predominantly Russian or Ukrainian.

So what did Amalia see around her as she grew up? What was shtetl culture like? Shtetls were small towns located mainly in the areas of the Pale of Settlement, created by Catherine II ('The Great') of Russia in 1791 under pressure to rid Moscow of Jewish business competitors and their 'evil' influence on the Russian masses. The Pale of Settlement covered parts of the Russian Empire, Poland, Galicia, and Romania; today this would include Lithuania, Belarus, Poland, Moldova, Ukraine, and parts of western Russia. Ninety per cent of Russian Jews were forced into the Pale, to live in poverty and hardship. Even then, they had to pay double the amount of taxes of ordinary citizens and were forbidden to own land, run taverns, or become properly educated. It is to their credit that Jewish communities prospered despite the discrimination against them – as evidenced in the expansion in their numbers from 1.6 million in 1820 to 5.6 million in 1910.

Some liberalisation in the treatment of Jews occurred in the mid-1800s, which led to some improvement to living conditions. This was reversed, however, some decades later when laws were passed in 1882 to impose further restrictions on Jews living within the Pale. At this time, in the 1870s and 1880s, the Jewish population also became the target of devastating pogroms –violent mob attacks against them, condoned by government and military authorities. Deteriorating living conditions and increased persecution combined to make emigration to other countries, even those that were far distant, attractive. The 1971 film *Fiddler on the Roof* provides a contemporary account of the pull-push factors of migration of Jews to the United States. Based on *Tevye and His Daughters* (also called *Tevye the Dairyman*) and other tales by Sholem Aleichem (1859–1916), a leading Yiddish author and playwright from Ukraine, the story centres on Tevye, the father of five daughters, and his attempts to maintain his family and Jewish religious traditions against the encroachment of external factors. Tevye copes both with the strong-willed actions of his three daughters—each one's choice of husband moving her further away from the customs of the Jewish faith – and the edict of the tsar to evict the Jews from the village. The film ends with the acceptance of alternative futures for Jewish people living in poverty, including political action, integration into non-Jewish communities, and migration to a safer place. Such factors led to the migration of two million Jews to America between 1881 and 1914, as well as increased interest in Zionism, which advocated the creation of a Jewish state. Restriction of Jews to the Pale of Settlement was eventually abolished only in 1917 following the Russian Revolution.

It is perhaps difficult today to understand why Jews were singled out as so threatening to Russian and later to German society, though many explanations have been offered and books written. Most believe that the roots of anti-Semitism lie in early biblical and religious disputes between Jews and Christians. The term anti-Semitism was first coined by an Austrian Jewish scholar Moritz Steinschneider in Germany in 1860, as a scientific term for what was previously understood as 'Judenhass' (Jew hatred). Steinschneider's aim was to highlight 'anti-Semitic prejudices' relating to the supposed inferiority of the 'Semitic races'. Such ideas about 'race' and civilization were widespread in Europe in the second half of the nineteenth century, and even in Britain, Jews were seen by many as racially inferior and culturally untrustworthy compared to the English, Scots, Welsh, and Irish. Different perceptions of Jewishness were evoked to create Jews as the 'other' or the outsider in relation to European societies. On the one hand, Eastern European Jews were regarded as poor, backward, overly religious, and a potential drain on more advanced Western European countries to which they sought entry. On the other hand, Western European Jews were castigated as wealthy and grasping plutocrats, whose main goals in life were to make money and take over the world. So, while Amalia's family might have felt secure in their shtetl home town of Brody, the world outside was becoming harsher for Jews. And their right to live lives similar to those of the rest of the population was again at risk.

Shtetl towns like Brody at the time of Amalia's birth were communities that followed traditional or Orthodox Judaism. They were largely stable, conservative, and socially inflexible. Amalia would be aware of the limitations placed on her, as a young woman. Men were in the dominant positions, controlling the organisation of religion and education, as well as commerce. Girls from poorer families faced bleak prospects, especially if they could not find a husband – although behind the scenes, women often played key roles in communal and economic life. There were some opportunities for girls to learn to read and write, with selected Yiddish religious and secular literature available to them, but overall the lives of girls and women were highly regulated and restrictive.[11] A typical shtetl town with Yiddish as its main language (a combination of Hebrew, German, Polish, and local dialects), Brody became known also for other things. For example, 'Brodersänger' (singers from Brody) were among the first to perform Yiddish songs in non-religious settings. The singers, akin to medieval troubadours, went from place to place, adapting their songs from religious music. They also acted as cantors in synagogues, that is, trained musicians leading the congregation in melodic prayer. The most noted Brodersängers were Berl Margulis (1815–1868) and Benjamin Wolf Ehrenkrantz (1826–1883), both mentioned mainly with disapproval by Jewish travellers passing through Brody. Amalia may well have attended one of Benjamin's concerts. More likely, she would have been forbidden to attend so ungodly an event.

The young Amalia may have developed her appreciation of music and performance from performers similar to these Jewish troubadours. When a mother herself, she would convey to her children, including my mother, her fondness for music and theatre.

A traveller in 1844 from Scotland describes Brody as a predominantly Jewish town, with 150 synagogues and prayer rooms and only 3 churches (2 Greek orthodox, 1 Roman Catholic). Brody is depicted as a near to ideal, settled, and thriving shtetl society:

> The streets in general are tolerably clean, and there is a side-pavement entirely of wood. The appearance of the population was certainly the most singular we had witnessed. It seemed wholly a Jewish city, and the few Gentiles who appeared here and there were quite lost in the crowd of Jews. Jewish boys and girls were playing in the streets and Jewish maid-servants carrying messages; Jewish women were the only females to be seen at the doors and windows; and Jewish merchants filled the market place. The high fur caps of the men, the rich head-dresses of the women, and the small round velvet caps of the boys met the eye on every side as we wandered from street to street. Jewish ladies were leaning over balconies, and poor old Jewesses were sitting at stalls selling fruit. In passing through the streets, if we happened to turn the head for a moment toward a shop, some Jew would rush out immediately and assail us with importunate invitations to come and buy. In the bazaar, Jews were selling skins, making shoes, and offering earthenware for sale; and the sign-boards of plumbers, masons, painters and butchers all bore Jewish names. In the fish market, the same kind of wrangling and squabbling heard in our own markets was carried on by Jewesses buying and selling. Jewesses

also presided at the flesh and poultry market and in a plentifully stored green-market...

> There are perhaps forty rich Jews in the city...but the greater part is poor... Most of the rising generation are giving up the study of the Talmud [book of Jewish laws], and several have been baptized. There is some learning among them; for in one synagogue we met with several lads who understood and spoke Hebrew. Many of the young men are beginning to attend the Government schools, in which they are taught Latin and acquire general knowledge. The rabbi of the New School speaks Latin and French. [12]

So, while Brody seemed to be a stable and flourishing Jewish community in 1844, new ideas and changes were in the air. The young and ambitious were beginning to reject Yiddish in favour of the national language, German, as well as French, and some were even giving up their Jewish faith altogether. Meanwhile others were setting their sights westwards towards the burgeoning cities of Central Europe and even America.

The noted European writer Joseph Roth, born in Brody in 1897 some twenty years after Amalia, argues that, generally, shtetl culture was underappreciated and wrongly dismissed, especially by those who had lived it. In his 1927 account of Jewish migrations from East to West following the First World War and the changes he witnessed in Russia, he wrote:

> Conversely, the Eastern Jew sees none of the advantages of his homeland. He sees nothing of the boundless horizon, nothing of the quality of the people, in whom simplicity can produce holy men and murderers, melodies of the melancholy, grandeur,

and obsessive passion... The Eastern Jew fails to see
the beauty of the East.[13]

I could find little information specific to Amalia's immediate
family. What documents exist suggest that the family name of her
father was Dinger, that of her mother was Moszkowicz, and that
she had at least one sister, Frieda (born 8 July 1877, and living with
the family in Vienna until 1942), and one brother, Sigmund (living
in 1899 in L'viv). Records show previous generations of the Dinger
family buried in the Brody graveyard. Other than that, there is little
more to say about Amalia's life or family in Brody. The hope is,
however, that the reader will have gained some sense of why Amalia
and her new husband may have wanted to leave their birthplace.

CHAPTER 4

Uszer in Poland, 1900–1923

The quotation at the beginning of this book by Ira Bruce Nadel is particularly apposite in the case of my father. It reads, 'The completeness of biography, the achievement of its professionalization, is an ironic fiction, since no life can ever be known completely.'

Uszer Frucht, also known by various other names (Usyer, Osher, Eddie, Edi, Frocht, and Frukht) was a complex and mysterious man, whose life spanned the first eight decades of the twentieth century and who was involved in many of the political and social movements that defined that era. For these reasons and also because he was a Jew, he was perpetually in the act of leaving, initially fleeing conscription in the Polish military and then as a persona non grata in Belgium and later facing expulsion from Britain because of his communist sympathies. It was only at the age of seventy-four, when he was at last granted citizenship in Belgium, that he was finally free of fear of arrest or deportation.

He was also my father, and his difficult relationship with governments and authority rendered him a ghostly and ephemeral presence throughout much of my early life. He had a long and enduring relationship with my mother yet he rarely saw her, corresponded with her sporadically, and spoke to her only occasionally by phone. They lived together in London for fewer than three years before he left the country, never to return on a permanent basis.

Nevertheless, he was a looming figure in my childhood, emotionally and physically. My mother loved him and wanted us to be with him, and he had a strong physical presence – bulky, ebullient, and exotic. There were planned meetings when my mother took me across the Channel to see him for a few days' holiday in Belgium or France. During the late 1940s and early 1950s, train travel was glamorous to a young child, particularly the ferry trains that went to the 'Continent'. I hugely enjoyed those trips. One joy I remember clearly was being served breakfast in the buffet car. It included *two* soft-boiled eggs served in a silver twin egg cup – this at a time when rationing was still in place in Britain. But primarily these trips meant spending special and exciting times with my mother. Being with my father was of less interest. One of my earliest memories is of him missing the train on which we three were booked, probably from Dieppe to Paris, as there is a photograph of the three of us together there. I recall that he rejoined the train at a later junction, but the moment of acute anxiety, presumably transmitted by my mother, has stayed with me throughout my life.

My father's irregular and spontaneous trips to see us in London were less agreeable. The first intimation of a visit would be a phone call to say he was on his way and to give the name of the ferry terminus or airport at which he would be arriving. All previous arrangements would be abandoned, which would cause havoc to our small, well-ordered lives. And though there was excitement (what presents might he bring this time?) there was a certain tension too. My mother became flustered and girlish, and I had to pretend that I was pleased to see him, even though I was fearful of his bulk and his smell and worried about disappointing him in some way or other. I was a large, noisy, ungainly child and had the impression that he would rather that his youngest daughter was quieter and more feminine.

As I grew older, I found it easier to romanticise about my father as a European hero who had suffered for his politics. The clothes he wore seemed glamorous in post-war London, in particularly his trench coat worn á la Humphrey Bogart, casually thrown over a well-cut foreign-looking double-breasted suit. He was multilingual, fluent in Yiddish, Polish, French, and Flemish, and his English was not at all bad either! We could communicate. I didn't much like having to touch his deformed thumb, though, or sitting too close to him. I coped as most children do concerning things over which they have no control, and I comforted myself with the thought that his stay would be only for a short time, and then he would go away again.

It was only after my mother died suddenly, when I was in my mid-twenties, then married with two young children, that I found out from my father that he had a fully grown first family in Belgium. It must have been when I asked him, during a fleeting visit to London sometime after my mother's funeral, about why he and my mother had never married, although I don't remember the exact occasion. I *do* remember asking him if he had told the Belgian family about me – us. He replied 'no' because as 'petty bourgeois', they would not understand. He was, however, sentimental about my young family and the additional grandchildren that he had never expected to have. Another time we went to see him in Ostend, and there are pictures of us walking along the beach and sitting in a restaurant, all trying so hard to get on.

But this visit was a failure, in the sense that I found that I could no longer handle the relationship. With my mother gone, perhaps the one person who could bind us together, and me still raw from losing her, I ceased corresponding with him and gradually excised him from my life. He kept on writing for a while. I have a short note from him urging me to write back. I did not, and contact fizzled out. I had no private address for him in Belgium, as all letters to him were addressed poste restante (in other words, sent to a collection point for letters) in Brussels. Presumably, when I moved house in the mid-1970s, he could no longer find me.

It was more than thirty years later in the early 2000s that I started to think about my father again, largely as an addendum to my investigation into my mother's escape to London from Nazi-occupied Vienna in 1938 and her eventual settlement in Britain. I knew the broad brushstrokes of her story but was never able to learn the details of what had happened. My mother's death in 1969 at the age of sixty-six had robbed me of my most knowledgeable informant. In exploring my mother's story, I was forced to think once more about my father and about how his life had affected hers and mine.

Initially, I sought the recollections of people who had known him however briefly. This included my now adult children, who had met him fleetingly when they were very young; my former husband; my Uncle John, who lived into his nineties; and several friends and distant relatives. I was also aided by the substantial file I found on him in the Belgian National Archive (file number 1256189), which provided details of his family origins and original reasons for entry into Belgium in 1923, as well as an overview of the main events of his subsequent life. This was a momentous discovery. It confirmed not only his material existence but also his personhood, that is, his interrelationships with others. Because he was an immigrant and the authorities were determined to keep track of him, the file included the minutiae of his life in Belgium, including identity card applications and notices of change of address, as well as police reports and formal documentation relating to his expulsion in 1939. Most were in French, some in Flemish. One document in English dated 1939 from the Home Office enquired whether he would be allowed back into Belgium if deported from the UK. Finally, the file contained details of his eventual achievement of Belgian citizenship in 1974. As important, the file included small passport-like photos (all new to me) documenting his changing appearance over the years.

The file also provided information on his 'first' family, including a half-brother, Henri, and two half-sisters, Clara and Augustine, which led me to the address where members of the family now lived in Brussels. The name Augustine Frucht was listed in the online Belgian telephone directory, and I discovered that this person was indeed my half-sister. A carefully written letter in schoolgirl French suggesting that we might have the same father, and enclosing photographs of me with my father in 1963, as well as my later family, gained an immediate response. A phone message confirmed that I had indeed found the right Augustine Frucht, that I was *effectivement* her sister, and that she would be delighted to meet me. She told me that her older half-brother, Henri, born in 1925, had recently died. Her sister, Clara, born in 1927, was alive and well and living in Brussels. Augustine, born in 1930 and the youngest in my father's first family, sounded strong and confident.

Following this encouraging response, I visited the family in Brussels twice in 2009 and received yet another perspective on my father, one at odds with the heroic picture that I had constructed thus far. I was taken to see his grave in the Brussels Jewish cemetery – and it was only then that I learnt the exact date of his death – the second momentous discovery. His wife was buried next to him, and I was startled by the jealousy I felt as I viewed her grave. Later, following a visit to Poland, I was able to obtain fragmentary details from the authorities about the Frucht family before and after the war, and learnt that many of Uszer's brothers and sisters and their families had perished in the Lodz Ghetto. Indeed, in a visa application in 1967 to attend a memorial ceremony at Auschwitz, my father stated that he had lost eighty family members in the Holocaust.

I found little reference to or documentation on him in Britain, where he lived between 1939 and 1946. The Home Office responded to an enquiry by stating that, whilst it had once held a file on Uszer Frucht, it had been destroyed sometime in the 1960s. The National Archive at Kew had nothing on Uszer Frucht or any of the other names he used, save a mention of him on a list of people scheduled for deportation in 1939, just before war broke out. In fact, hostilities began before the action could be carried out. My mother's National Archive file contains several references to him as Mr Frocht, mostly disapproving. The more accommodating Association of Jewish Refugees (AJR)[14] forwarded to me a copy of a record card noting his imprisonment in Lewes jail in 1948, near the channel port of Newhaven.

It was evident that his wartime political activities did not attract the attention of the British authorities even though he was an active member of the Soviet-inspired Jewish Cultural Club which was both a conduit during the war for information between Moscow and London and a fundraiser for sending provisions to the Russian Front. On 27 April 1942, for example, the JCC announced, 'London to Broadcast May First Message to Jewish Workers in Poland':

> A message of encouragement to the Jewish workers in Nazi-held Poland will be broadcast from here in Yiddish on Friday, May 1st, by Samuel Zygelhaum, the Jewish labour member of the Polish National Council.

> In preparation for May Day which Jewish and non-Jewish labour organisations will observe here under the slogan of "all possible aid to Soviet Russia in the fight against Nazism," the Jewish Cultural Club of London today issued an appeal to the Jews of Great Britain to establish a committee composed of representatives of leading Jewish groups for the purpose of organising maximum aid for Russia's war effort.[15]

After the war, members met regularly and remained friends until 1956, when splits occurred following the Hungarian Uprising.[16]

On the actual date of my birth (9 May 1944), Srebnik reports, Uszer was down to speak at a conference in Beaver Hall, Stepney, organised by the East London District of the Communist Party, on persuading Jews to join the Communist Party.[17] From such fragmentary sources, as well as from accounts of the social and political times he lived through, during what Eric Hobsbawm has referred to as 'The Age of Extremes'[18], I have attempted to 'author' a narrative of my father's life, and this is what follows.

Uszer Frucht was born in Lodz in what is now Central Poland. The year of his birth is generally given as 1900, although I grew up thinking that he had been born a year later. When he first arrived in Belgium (as Ensel rather than Uszer) for reasons we shall learn about later, his birth date was given as 1897. However, 1900 is the date on his Brussels' tombstone. Perhaps that is the most reliable source of evidence.

The year of Uszer's birth is confirmed in his birth certificate, hand-written in 'old' Russian. An approximate translation is as follows:

The city of Lodz, 19 January

Gershek Yankel Frokht (age 38, weaver by occupation, permanent resident of the city of Lodz) arrived on 1 February 1902 at 10.00 a.m. In the presence of Gabriel Segal (age 35), Moshka Kalinski (age 35) and Abraham Aster (age 52)…and introduced the mother of the male child, confirming that he had been born in the city of Lodz on 27 September 1900 at 11.00 a.m. to his wife Sura Rukhlya (née Brusechinskaya, age 36). The child had been given, by birth, the name of Ushery.

This act was read to us and signed…

It is interesting to see that the birth was notified to the authorities a year and a half after the event. According to the birth certificate, Uszer (or Ushery) was born a week before his officially credited birthday (20 September 1900). Perhaps this was a clerical error, perhaps not! Other records confirm his parents as Herszek Jankiel Frocht [19] (born 1862) and Sura Ruchla Brzezinska (born 1864), who lived all their lives in or near Lodz. They died in their late sixties so lived to see the high point of Lodz's history for the Jewish population. At the time of my father's birth in 1900, Lodz had the second largest population of Polish Jews after Warsaw and was one of the largest Jewish communities in the world.

His parents were poor, and he had a number of siblings. Records suggest that many of them died in the Lodz Ghetto. The following brothers and sisters have been identified: Abram Frocht (1889–1942), Majer Frocht (1890–1942, died on transport from Lodz), Symcha Mojsze Frocht (1894–1922), Tauba Frocht, (1906–1940/4, died in Lodz Ghetto), and Chaja Frocht (1919–?). Another brother, Moritz, travelled to France at the same time as Uszer headed for Belgium. No more information is available. Uszer's father is described as a weaver on the birth certificate, and it is likely that the men and perhaps some women in the family were involved in textile production, most likely in small workshops rather than larger factories, which tended not to employ Jews. The women in the family had prime responsibility for looking after the children and menfolk and for keeping the home going. There was a whisper within the Belgian branch of the family of a rabbi somewhere in the family history – but perhaps such a rumour has an echo in most Jewish families.

Lodz (Łódź), the city of Uszer's birth, is yet another town with a long history. It first appeared in a 1332 document granting possession of the village of Łodzia to the Polish bishops of Włocławek. City rights were awarded in 1423, and for the next four centuries, Lodz remained a small urban mark on the trade route between Masovia in central Poland and Silesia on the German border. Following the

1815 Congress of Vienna, the city was absorbed into the Russian Empire, and the now dilapidated metropolis became a target for rebuilding and renewal. The tsar gave permission for German-based companies to clear the land for house and factory building and so transform it into a modern industrial textile centre. The city prospered over the next decades, attracting migrants from all over Europe. These settlers came mainly from Southern Germany but also from Portugal, England, France, and Ireland. The first cotton mill and steam-powered factory in the city opened in 1825 and 1839 respectively, and a German industrialist Karl Scheibler built the city's first cotton-spinning mill in the mid-1850s. Three groups dominated the city's population at this time – Germans, who were in the majority, Poles and Jews who had started to arrive in appreciable numbers from 1848 onwards. The city's population doubled each decade between 1823 and 1873, with the period of most intense industrial development between 1870 and 1890, when Jews made up around a third of the population.[20]

The first Jewish presence in Lodz was noted in 1775, some four hundred years after its foundation, when a publican, Joachim Zelkowicz, and his wife, were recorded as managing 'the brewery of the city' where they also lived.[21] Numbers increased only slowly, from twelve in 1791 to ninety-eight (grouped in twenty-five families) in 1809. By this time, the community felt sufficiently secure to purchase land for a Jewish cemetery, and in 1811, a wooden synagogue was constructed in the centre of town. This was to collapse several times before eventually being rebuilt in brick in 1863 – a year after Uszer's father's birth. The Jewish population of Lodz gradually increased, due mainly to involvement in trade with Russia and in textile production – as artisans, workers, and small and middling factory owners. Eventually the medieval (Jewish) ghetto could no longer contain the volume of population and Jews spread to other parts of the city.

They were granted full public rights in Poland in 1862, which benefitted the existing population but also helped attract Jews facing persecution in other countries. They first came to Lodz from other parts of Poland and then from Russia from 1882 onwards, following pogroms and a series of expulsions by the tsar. A decade later, Jews were dominant in Lodz textile manufacture and also highly visible in international trade. Similar to developments in Vienna at the time, the Jewish community was much involved in the arts, theatre, literature, journalism, education, and so on – in other words, in the cultural and intellectual life of the city. We have already seen the example of the Poznanski Palace built in Lodz by a wealthy Jewish textile industrialist.

Its industrial nature meant that Lodz was, perhaps inevitably, a major centre of revolutionary politics. For example, in 1892 a widely supported strike calling for higher wages brought the factories to a halt. In 1905, an insurrection resulted in the deaths of hundreds of workers. Uszer's childhood in the first decade of the twentieth century would, therefore, necessarily have been influenced by both the confident and flourishing Jewish presence in the city and, given he was from a poor family, the revolutionary fervour swirling around him, in particular following the Russian Revolution in 1917.

By Uszer's teens, Lodz had developed into one of the most densely populated industrial cities in the world. An immensely important centre for textile production, it was known as the 'Polish Manchester', although this status was to change dramatically with the onset of war in 1914.

While Poland did not exist as an independent state during the First World War, its geographical position between the fighting powers meant that much military action and huge human losses occurred on Polish territory. At the start of the war, Polish territory was split between the Austro-Hungarian, German, and Russian Empires, and so it was the scene of many skirmishes and battles on what was known as the Eastern Front.

Following a major battle close by in the first year of the war, Lodz was occupied by the Germans until eventually liberated by the Polish Army in 1918. The years after 1918 were difficult for the newly independent Poland and for the city. I imagine Uszer as young man walking the streets of Lodz, excited and motivated by the possibilities of what could be won for the workers and his fellow Jews following the example of the Russian Revolution, but also dispirited by growing poverty, nationalism, and anti-Semitism in his own country.

At the end of the war, Lodz lost approximately 40 per cent of its inhabitants, first through the casualties of war and then as the German-speaking population was 'repatriated' to Germany and, finally, due to emigration. It was sometime during this period that Uszer took the decision to leave Lodz, possibly with a brother Moritz. He headed initially for Germany and then, later, for the coalfields of Charleroi in Belgium. He may have been an out-of-work textile worker or may have already worked as a miner nearer home, perhaps in the coalfields of Silesia towards the west.

The precise reason or reasons he decided to leave are unknown, as he left no papers or testimony. Reasons suggested by his Belgian family vary. Among these are his desire to escape from the religious, narrow parochialism of Lodz Jewish family life of the time, avoidance of an arranged marriage, a search for work at a time when Lodz was entering a period of economic decline, fear of anti-Semitic pogroms, and so on. However, the most likely reason, borne out by later searches for him in Belgium by the Polish military, was threat of military conscription into the Polish Army, which could last for up to twenty-five years and/or the fines demanded for failure to comply.

Broader factors also influenced Uszer's decision to leave Lodz, primarily to do with his politics. First, there was the political fallout from the Russian Revolution and the victory of the Bolsheviks in the Civil War that followed. As the new Soviet state began to turn its attention westwards, the next step was to secure Poland for Bolshevism, which would then act as a gateway for further revolutionary gains in Western Europe, particularly Germany.[22] Among the most responsive to the call were young urban, male Jews like Uszer who, for the reasons above, were disproportionately active in supporting early forms of Bolshevism, though they constituted but a small minority of the Jewish population overall.[23] This group, therefore, was viewed as a particular menace by the new Polish state.

A study of Polish Jewish communists born around 1910, about a decade later than Uszer, suggests that the allure of revolution to young Jews was none of the above but was associated primarily with youthful revolt against their families and, presumably, rejection of traditional, conservative Jewish practices.[24] Whatever the nature of their radicalism, their degree of assimilation, or their views on the relationship between Judaism and politics, the majority's main concern was to reject the world of their parents. As a recent historian summarised,

> Whether they came from poor, more prosperous, assimilated or traditional families, an important common element in their situation was an intense perception of the difference separating them from their parents. Increasingly experienced as unbridgeable, expressed on the everyday level as an inability to communicate and a refusal to conform, these differences led them increasingly to distance themselves from the world, ways, and values of their parents.[25]

One reason for Uszer's departure then might have been rejection of his parents' more devout and less political generation. As for his expectation of being conscripted into the Polish Army, notoriously anti-Semitic[26], the need to escape became more urgent when war broke out between the country of his birth, Poland, and the country of his aspirations, the Soviet Union. We do not know whether he left before or after receiving his call-up papers. Either way, the pending conscription was a key factor in his decision to leave. His birth into a large, poor, Yiddish-speaking Jewish household; his lack of schooling; and the limited nature of any future for him in the newly independent and increasingly anti-Semitic Polish state provided added incentives.

It is not known why he decided to go West rather than East to the Soviet Union, as did some comrades. Perhaps he was following relatives or was sent as an advance guard to plant the seeds of the revolution in Europe. A prime reason was likely economic. He found out somehow that good jobs were to be had in the coalfields of Germany and Belgium, perhaps through active recruitment by mining companies or a supportive comradely grapevine. The havoc created by the First World War, massive loss of life in the trenches, and post-war economic recovery had led to a shortage of workers across Europe. France and Belgium became a particular magnet for Eastern European economic migrants, many of whom were also political exiles. Indeed, they came in the thousands to work in western European coalfields.[27] One of these was Uszer, who left Poland around 1922, never to return.[28]

CHAPTER 5

Steffi in Vienna, 1903–1938

The third of the triumvirate of lives in this book is that of my mother. Like her mother Amalia, her life had distinct phases – the first half was spent growing up and working in the exciting cultural and political milieu of pre-war Vienna. Later, we follow her to London, initially as a German-speaking refugee, and then as a single mother and as a hardworking and respectable, if not officially designated, British citizen. Not only did she endure and survive the murderous impulses of Nazism following the German sweep into Vienna in March 1938, but also, unbeknown to her, she suffered the attention of the post-war British secret services, which colluded to deny her the possibility of British citizenship and ultimate security. In telling her story, I explore, as with Amalia's and Uszer's stories, the degree to which her life mirrors that of the many caught up in the waves of humanity scattered about the globe in the twentieth century and the extent to which she was able to take autonomous decisions about her own and other people's lives, including mine as her daughter. When tragedy struck, she was able to escape and make a new life for herself. In throwing her lot in with others who were similarly traumatised and who had their beliefs in the future shattered, however, she was rendered vulnerable once more, this time, by the shadow of Cold War politics. That said, her sixty-six years of life can also be seen as a breath-taking cultural journey, starting out in the dying embers of the Hapsburg Empire and ending in London's Swinging Sixties.

In her youth, Steffi was hopeful about her future. She had beauty, intelligence, and modernity on her side, and she was born into one of the great twentieth-century European cultural centres, Vienna. Stefanie (Steffi) Dinger was born on 19 January 1903 in Vienna to Amalia and David Dinger, both originally from Brody in Galicia. We have seen that her parents moved from their remote shtetl birthplace to the centre of the Austro-Hungarian Empire to seek their fortunes, escape anti-Semitism, and gain a toehold in a modern city. Initially, they were successful on all three fronts. In the end, they failed in all of them.

Steffi was the couple's third daughter, coming after their firstborn, Malvine, who died in infancy and her older sister by two years, Gisela. For much of her life, Steffi was the second oldest of her siblings and took her seniority seriously. She was an attractive child, with an equable and friendly nature. Those who knew her remarked frequently on her warmth, charm, and good looks – indeed, there is a family story that she was once stopped in the street by an artist who begged to have the chance to paint her. However, there is no trace or photograph of the painting among the family papers, so perhaps the story is apocryphal.

The first decade of Steffi's life took place in the last years of the Hapsburg Empire. The era of her birth was a time of great artistic and cultural efflorescence for Vienna, the empire's epicentre. One example of this sparkling cultural climate was the secessionist movement, which was formed by nineteen artists in the late 1890s as a generational rebellion against the historical or 'traditional' styles predominant among European painters at the time. Gustav Klimt was the Vienna Secession's first president, and he and others in the group, including Klimt's protégé, Egon Schiele, developed new portrayals of the human body and new interpretations of art nouveau involving rich ornamentation and vivid colour. This was a time of advancement and modernity with an emphasis, nonetheless, on the eternal artistic targets of beauty and splendour – exemplified in Klimt's striking use of metallic gold and silver in the background to his figures. The style epitomised fin-de siècle Vienna – innovation and modernity intersected with sentimentality and indulgence. It denoted a culture and society that seemed unaware of, and perhaps regarded itself as impervious to, the huge changes and disintegration that were to follow.

The first decade of the twentieth century was also a time of emigration to Vienna from other parts of the Hapsburg Empire. Documents from the 1910 census reveal that Vienna's population was large for the period, just over two million, and exceptionally diverse. Only about half of its citizens were Viennese born. The rest travelled in from rural Austria and other parts of the Empire, for example,

Bohemia, Moravia, Hungary, Galicia (like the Dingers), Silesia, and also Germany. Vienna was thus a city of recent multilingual arrivals, more so as the First World War broke out in 1914, and Polish and Yiddish-speaking refugees arrived to escape fighting on the Eastern Front. As shortages and austerity became commonplace, the response of many Viennese was to blame the incomers rather than the authorities, more so for exacerbating a climate of hostility and suspicion.

Jews formed only five per cent of the overall Austro-Hungarian population; however, they were overwhelmingly concentrated in Vienna and were, thus, visible and vulnerable. In the decades before 1914, Viennese Jews tended to cluster in the inner city (District 1) and Leopoldstadt (District 2), where the Dingers lived. The wealthy inhabited the avenues, the middle classes, the side streets, and the poor, the back alleys.[29] I would judge that the Dingers belonged to the lower end of the middle grouping. Before the war, Jews had been active in imperial and city life, socially and intellectually as well as financially, and were visible out of all proportion to their numbers.[30] They came to the public eye in a wide range of areas of cultural life, and for some, Jewish influence seemed everywhere. Following the celebrity of Sigmund Freud and Alfred Adler, the noted Jewish cultural critic Karl Kraus commented, tongue-in-cheek, 'The Jews control the press, they control the stock-market, and now they also control the unconscious.'[31]

Politically, the Austro-Hungarian dual monarchy with its two autonomous parliaments in Vienna and Prague began to run out of steam mid-nineteenth century. Initially inspired by the 1848 revolutions throughout Europe, various under-represented nationalities in the Empire, for example, Slovaks, Czechs, Romanians, Serbs, and Croats, struggled to establish their own autonomous states. These aims were finally realised after the defeat of the Empire in 1918. A commentator writing some decades later summarises the outcome cogently:

> In 1918 the polyglot monarchy, with its banknotes printed in eight different languages, broke up by virtue of centrifugal forces. Its subject races departed each to its own next of kin. Czechs and Slovaks founded Czechoslovakia, Serbs and Croats Jugoslavia, 'Old' Rumanians and Transylvanians Greater Rumania. [All that] remained [was] the compact bloc of Magyars [Hungarians] in the centre (who also broke away from the Austrians) and Austria itself.[32]

The consequence of this upheaval was the creation of different nation states on the basis of 'blood-tie' and ethnic 'belonging', simultaneous to the decline of the multinational, super state, governed bureaucratically from the centre, which whatever its faults, had offered protection to minorities. The Jewish community as a whole had been grateful for the role that Emperor Franz Joseph had played in their political, social, and cultural emancipation and so were loyal citizens in the fight to protect the empire and the German-speaking world.

The era surrounding Steffi's birth thus saw the settled modernity of many Viennese citizens and their pride in the cultural and political influence of Vienna. It also coincided with the growth of nationalism(s), anti-Semitism, and political instability as various national groups sought independence. No doubt Steffi's parents were aware of the wider forces beyond their growing family in Leopoldstadt, but they were probably more focused on getting food into the mouths of their children and inserting themselves in the local economy. Other children were born in 1905, 1906, and 1909. The family was completed by a daughter Gertrude (Trude) born in 1917, though two children died in infancy, presumably casualties of the long-term effects of what came to be known as 'total' war.[33]

The notion of total war is an interesting one. It was first applied to the conflict of 1914 to 1918 but later became identified with twentieth-century battlegrounds and into the twenty first century. It moves away from a concept of war involving only military and other fighting forces to recognition of the impact of modern warfare that incorporates both military and civilian populations and that does not differentiate between losses at the front and so-called collateral damage suffered by civilians. Total war in 1914 meant, therefore, that the civilian population as much as the military was expected to contribute to the war effort, with the state supreme in the sense that 'no action or deed is too small or significant to be considered a matter of state'.[34] Thus, as the Hapsburg Empire slid into war in 1914, mobilising military and civilian populations became paramount, astutely sustained by propaganda and jingoism.

Steffi was eleven years old when war broke out. At the beginning, the family supported the war effort like everyone else. As recent immigrants with a Jewish background, they were especially grateful to the empire for the improvement in their lives thus far. They were also confident that their side would win, as was the rest of the population. With most menfolk at the front, women like Steffi's mother and her aunt and men beyond military age like her father were expected to uphold the key wartime principles of sacrifice and 'holding out'. Anything deemed pleasurable was subsumed to stoicism, hard work, and 'making do'. Steffi was encouraged to contribute actively to the national patriotic effort, for instance, by writing and drawing and painting pictures depicting what the war meant to her, thus helping carry the war mentality into the schoolroom.

It was only later, as starvation and suffering hit the city, that support for the war faltered. I remember tales of hunger during these years and the family's almost total dependence, as I recall, on potatoes, often inedible. Queuing was a particular hardship. Scarcity of the basic staples led to endless waiting in line and much squabbling and hostility, all of which created an atmosphere of paranoia and denunciation. The creeping impact of total war and the combined effects of hunger and exhaustion began to take their toll. There was competition over who got what and who was most deserving or important, not only in relation to the two main countries in the empire, Austria and Hungary, but between city and rural dwellers, between those at home and at the front, and between the deserving and undeserving. Scarcity of food poisoned neighbourly relations so much so that anyone who seemed better fed was viewed with suspicion, as were those who were seen to put personal or family interests above those of the empire. Poorer incomers like the Dingers were the most likely to go without. As we know, two babies in the Dinger family died during this time, and Trude, the one surviving child born in wartime, was malnourished and suffered poor health throughout her relatively short life.

Any perceived selfishness was designated 'un-Austrian', a disturbing concept for Jewish families. I know that my mother felt utterly Austrian as well as Jewish and, indeed, was a huge admirer of German literature and culture. Yet, if 'un-Austrian' could be applied to strangeness of attitude and behaviour and/or lack of Austrian ethnic nationality, it did not take much imagination to see where this might lead – to the perception of the Jewish community as inherently un-Austrian. The influence of nationalism increased throughout the war with a resultant lingering distrust of foreigners as the war came to a close. A fear of the future that all Viennese citizens shared was exacerbated for those living in the poorer Jewish areas by violently anti-Semitic gangs of scavengers and looters, for whom they were particularly enticing targets.

The Hapsburg Empire had been routed. Early defeats in battle had a devastating effect. For example, in the first six months of fighting, three-quarters of a million Austrian soldiers were lost, including a high percentage of the officer class. Later victories over Russia and Italy helped restore the army's reputation. However, it was largely external factors that were to seal Austria's fate. First, the Russian Revolution in 1917 provided inspiration for Polish, Czech, and Yugoslavian calls for independence. Second, the German allies' defeat in 1918 provided the preconditions for the empire's collapse. Austria was reduced to a rump, a small German-speaking state with shrunken borders and a grandiose capital. Over the four years of war, the city of Vienna experienced increased social disintegration, as little formal machinery existed for imposing social order. There were few mechanisms, for instance, for resolving conflict between people of different ethnic, religious, and political groups – previously, recognition of empire had been the primary cohesive force. Moreover, with the empire gone and abject in defeat, Austrians became restless and resentful of the absolutism of wartime military rule and the consequent lack of freedom and democracy. If that was not enough, the year 1918 experienced an exceptionally harsh winter, calamitous crop failure, and a global influenza epidemic that targeted the young and healthy. Among its victims was the painter Gustav Klimt's young and promising disciple, Egon Schiele.

So, how did the Dinger family respond to the ups and downs of the military campaign and the hardships that followed? They certainly became more critical of their leaders as defeat beckoned and as conditions within the city deteriorated. The Jewish community, itself, organised support for the poorest and neediest of its members and was particularly active in welcoming and supporting injured soldiers arriving home from the front. My mother rarely talked about this period. Neither did she mention the loss of the two infants; perhaps it was a dark time that she wanted to put behind her.

The politicians running Austria after the war were not the same as those who had been there at the beginning. Social Democrats were now in power, not Hapsburg imperialists. With no model for a non-imperial Austria (the empire had existed in one form or another since 1279), however, the new regime was reaching into the unknown. It was decided to name the new Austria Deutschösterreich (the German-Austrian Republic) in the hope that Austria's six million German speakers would eventually be joined to the newly democratic Germany. But this was vetoed by the war's victors, who, perhaps wisely, were fearful of creating a power stretching from Hungary and Italy to the Baltic Sea. Without anything positive to hope for, Vienna sunk into chaos and misery. In 1919, the city's chief medical officer reported that 130,000 men were unemployed and more than 20,000 children were close to starvation, including as we know, those in the Dinger family. Moreover, the currency was collapsing, one violent demonstration followed another, and people were dying in the streets – from bullets, fists, or hunger.

Despite or because of this, Viennese preoccupation with the 'enemy within' continued long after the end of the war. The same groups that had been accused of poor attitude and lack of patriotism continued to be targets for hostility afterwards, now with added violence. The Jewish community, which had been supportive of the imperial monarchy during the war, was now blamed, at least in part, for the chaos that followed. The repercussions were long-standing and divisive: 'Anti-Slavic and anti-Semitic groups sought to secure the German, Christian character of Vienna in much more violent ways than they had prior to 1914. In the periodization of Austrian history, the war years provide the bookend to the imperial era, but they also mark the starting point for the violence and disorder of the interwar years.'[35]

Whatever perils they faced, Steffi and the other Dinger children attended and benefited from elementary education before and during the war, followed by attendance at Realschule, a form of secondary school in Germany and Austria that emphasised the vocational and practical. From Realschule, they could go on to the more academic Gymnasium in preparation for university, vocational college, or straight into work. Following Realschule, Steffi attended a form of secretarial college. Thereafter, she worked as an administrator and bookkeeper for various companies in Vienna, before she lost her job in 1938 alongside other Jewish workers, a few months after the Nazis entered Austria.

Few photographs or documents, excepting certificates of birth and deaths, exist from the early period of Steffi's life. However, kept among her possessions and therefore of much significance for her, is a fine leather-covered autograph book containing inscriptions, poems, and pictures written and drawn by her siblings and friends, starting in 1915, with the last entry dated 1923. The book was a twelfth birthday present and included watercolour sketches and a poem from a friend, Erna Max, dated 1915, alongside inscriptions from a couple of her teachers, Elsa Braun, dated 1916, and Hermine Walter, dated 1917. One of the last entries, in 1923, is from Cilli Berlin, who describes herself as a friend from work (Bürakollegin).

From this album, we can see that Steffi had a wide range of friends, as well as enjoying good relationships with her siblings, if the warm inscriptions from her sisters and brother are to be believed. All this suggests that, even during the toughest of times, the Dinger family sought to maintain the niceties of social life.

The photographs we have of Steffi and other members of her family from this period show another side of the austerity of the post-war period – a solid home base, a recovery of spirits, and a delight in the aesthetic. For instance, the photograph below shows Steffi at about sixteen years old, her younger sister Elsa, and their maternal uncle Sigmund, of whom we shall see more later.

A later photograph below shows a rather glamorous seventeen-year-old Steffi, perhaps celebrating the end of her college education and is clearly a studio portrait. However, with the invention of the Kodak Brownie camera in 1900, later photographs of holidays and family gatherings show greater informality.

Interestingly, it was an Austrian, Joseph August Lux, who championed the use of the Brownie for its cultural potential. He argued in 1908 that it would enable ordinary 'amateurs' to photograph and document their surroundings and thus produce a form of stability among the challenges and insecurities of the modern world.[36] Non-studio photographs of Steffi and her friends and family appear towards the end of the 1920s, when the handheld camera became affordable for (upper) working-class families.

By the 1920s, Steffi was at work, contributing to the family income and retaining some of her wages for her own personal use, as presumably was Gisela, her older sister, later followed by Moritz, Elsa, Tilda, and Trude. She retained a great love of German literature and of the theatre and cinema until the day she died (the actress Greta Garbo was a big heroine of hers). Going out for coffee and cake at the weekend, a Viennese tradition, was one of my remembered childhood treats – even if, in London in the 1950s, the quality of the experience might not have been the same. Travel was also possible for Steffi in the 1920s, mainly by railway. We know that Steffi took a number of business as well as holiday trips to Budapest, Rotterdam, and Amsterdam from her photograph albums and the hotel labels pressed into her autograph book.

By the second half of the decade, she was enjoying the life of a modern independent woman, with friends and family in attendance. Steffi continued to take holidays in other parts of Austria and in Hungary and for work, as indicated by her professional outfit in the 1934 Budapest snap below. By the mid-1930s, she was clearly living the good life, as a mature young woman, seemingly with little need or desire to 'settle down'.

Male friends seemed part of Steffi's life throughout. Indeed, a fiancé, as my mother referred to him, appears in photographs between 1933 and 1938 – in Brody, the original Dinger hometown, in 1933 and enjoying a good social life with Steffi and her family in Vienna later. However, I was never told this suitor's name. Nor did I learn what happened to him. I had assumed he had died before the war, as there is, among my mother's belongings, a 1936 postcard showing him resident in Piestary, a spa town in what is now Slovakia, where he had seemingly gone for treatment or convalescence, for TB or something similar.

However more recently, I was sent by the AJR (Association of Jewish Refugees) an undated record card showing that an Ignatz Gold from Vienna had enquired after Steffi Dinger at the end of the war. The name made little sense to me until I had another look at one of the photographs of Steffi's fiancé, this one dated 16 October 1938. It had a scribbled name on the back – which I could now decipher as Ignatz Gold.

Here was another piece in the puzzle of my mother's life; Ignatz Gold was the name of my mother's Viennese fiancé. The 1938 photograph above was possibly a parting gift from him as she left for London. Although Steffi must have been informed by the AJR of Ignatz's enquiry, I do not know if she responded, and I have no memory of his name or of meeting him. Internet searches have yielded no further information, and now it is too late to ask anyone else, although my American cousin George, only two years old when war broke out, has some distant memory of the name cropping up in family discussions.

However, one can only imagine Steffi's feelings of turmoil when Ignatz made contact – joy that he was alive certainly but also fear that her pre-war Viennese suitor might damage the fragile post-war liaison that she had developed with Uszer.

The Vienna of the 1920s and early 1930s, still to all intents a world metropolis with an imposing facade of imperial splendour, was beneath fractured and fearful. Older citizens tried to preserve the Victorian atmosphere of Emperor Franz-Josef's era. For example, George Clare recounts that his Jewish grandmother was content to live in shabby and old-fashioned comfort.[37] The older generation of Dingers was less prosperous and less westernised than Clare's grandmother, perhaps more like his aunt Adele from Galicia whose speech was punctuated by 'never-ending sighs' and worried looks. This generation seemed happier focusing on Austria's splendid past than on its uncertain future.

Steffi's younger generation was more hopeful. As a child growing up in Vienna in the 1920s, the historian Eric Hobsbawm recalls that he did not experience anti-Semitism personally. Brought up in a non-religious household, he felt entirely remote from traditional forms of Judaism on which so much prejudice was based. As far as I can recollect from my mother, this was the same for the Dinger children. They were proud to be citizens of Austria and residents of Vienna. Yet, however modern and progressive they aspired to be, it was important for them to acknowledge their Jewish identity. Indeed, Hobsbawm remembers his mother telling him very firmly that he must never do anything or seem to do anything that might suggest that he was ashamed of being a Jew.[38] Heightened anti-Semitism brought with it fear and apprehension but also greater ethnic awareness and solidarity.

The photographs of Steffi and her friends above give little indication of the anxieties and pressures they may have felt as Austria moved towards fascism in the 1930s. Indeed, they could not be expected to have an inkling of what was to come. Austria was not Germany after all, and Kurt von Schuschnigg, the Austrian chancellor between 1934 and 1938, clearly expressed his opposition both to Hitler's ambitions to absorb Austria into the Third Reich and to overt anti-Semitism. The nature of Schuschnigg's power base was a worry, however, because it included the pseudo-military organisation, Heimwehr (Home Guard), a fascist militia modelled on the force created by Mussolini. After Hitler's accession to the chancellorship of Germany in 1933, violence escalated in Vienna, underground Nazi cells planted bombs in Jewish shops, anti-Semitism became more overt, and Nazi support grew exponentially.

The Dingers, like most other Jews were Social Democratic Party members, and indeed that is what Steffi emphatically stated when accused in the 1950s of having communist sympathies. The Social Democratic Party was preferred because the Jewish community tended towards the liberal side of politics and because the Social Democrats formed the main opposition to anti-Semitism. Many of the Social Democrat leaders were themselves Jewish or of Jewish origin. When the party came to power in 1918, they had been determined to oppose fascism, as well as put poverty and the humiliation of defeat behind them. In so doing, they sought social transformation by promoting socially progressive policies.

Opportunities for Social Democratic policymaking were short-lived, however. The post-war coalition broke down in 1920, and from then until 1945, the Social Democrats at the national level were either the official opposition or, later, a proscribed organisation. They continued, however, in power in Vienna for more than a decade, where their influence was more persistent. In this instance, their main purpose was to demonstrate what an enlightened city politics could achieve by, for example, creating housing schemes for the working classes alongside newly-built schools kindergartens, libraries, and hospitals; passing social insurance legislation; and imposing rent controls. The largest housing complex in Vienna, Karl Marx Hof, was designed to provide living quarters for five thousand people and included laundries, baths, kindergartens, doctors' surgeries, and a library. This social programme dubbed 'Red Vienna' became famous throughout the world as an example of the possibility of socialist reform without the need of revolution. However, such policies had their detractors, not least Austrian right-wing clergy, who labelled them 'godless and Jewish-Bolshevist'.[39]

Steffi and her family prospered from the policies of Red Vienna. Economic conditions gradually improved for them so that, in 1924, the family was able to move to a rented apartment in a more upmarket part of Leopoldstadt, no doubt aided by the imposed rent freeze. They also benefited from free medical services and the availability of parks, public baths, and sports venues, all designed to encourage their fitness and health.

Outside the urban areas, people were more conservative and resentful of what they saw as the overly radical politics of city leaders. Rural political groupings competed with each other to show their support for anti-Semitism. The Peasant League, for example, maintained that Judaism was Austria's real enemy and so attacked the Agrarian League for using an insurance company with Jewish directors. Similarly, the ruling Christian Social Party criticised Jewish influence in Austrian politics and blamed Jewish Social Democrat leaders for the destruction of Austrian traditions. The freedom to express such views had become familiar and 'normal' to Jews over the decades, but their continued articulation nevertheless led to heightened levels of anxiety and isolation.

Vienna itself had a history of anti-Semitism, even if its politics tended to be more progressive than the surrounding areas. In 1897, an anti-Semitic 'rabble-rouser' Karl Lueger was appointed mayor against the wishes of the Emperor Franz Joseph.[40] A zealous Catholic who wished to 'capture the university' for the Church, Lueger refused to allow either Social Democrats or Jews to join his municipal administration. The model of social progress he adopted, though 'modernistic', was bolstered by anti-Semitic rhetoric. It, thus, foreshadowed the stance adopted by Adolf Hitler decades later, when Lueger was acknowledge as a major influence on the creation of the Third Reich. Lueger advocated policies of discrimination against non-German speaking minorities across the Austro-Hungarian Empire and, in 1887, supported a bill to restrict the immigration of Russian and Romanian Jews. He also overtly supported movements to eliminate the supposed Jewish domination of the Hungarian capital, Budapest.

Lueger's municipal ambitions for Vienna were more progressive, and this is what he is celebrated for nowadays. For example, he is credited with modernising the city's water, gas, and electricity supplies, as well as creating a comprehensive public transport system and establishing parks and gardens, hospitals, and schools. During his tenure of thirteen years, which lasted until his death in 1910, Vienna became the modernised capital of a great imperial power – a legacy that continued in the developments of Red Vienna. Significantly, with the widening of the franchise, Lueger was one of the first local politicians to adopt populism as a political strategy, with his rhetorical anti-Semitic stance, some have argued, mainly aimed at securing the popular vote. In actuality, it is said, his administration was largely democratic and fair.[41]

Thus, even as the politics of Red Vienna in the 1920s were admired as progressive and modern, anti-Semitism was never far away. The Social Democrat regime in Vienna came to an abrupt end in 1927 as conservatives intensified their attacks on Red Vienna policies. In July of that year, angry protesters set the Justizpalast ablaze after the acquittal in Vienna of three right-wing paramilitaries on trial for murdering two demonstrators against a nationalist paramilitary march. A furious crowd stormed the University on Ringstrasse, attacking a police station and newspaper building on the way, before proceeding to Parliament. In the ensuing chaos, the police opened fire on the crowd, killing eighty-nine people and injuring more than five hundred. The Social Democrats condemned the action, calling for a general strike and the sacking of the chief of police. The country seemed on the verge of civil war, yet momentarily the Social Democratic leadership hesitated to act.[42]

The government moved in to break the strike and restore order, with the help of the Mussolini-inspired Heimwehr. Neither the police chief nor the police force faced criminal charges for what had been a disastrous turn of events. The reluctance of the Viennese Social Democrats to take action provided an opportunity for the national government to strengthen its power base. In 1929, a series of parliamentary acts restricting the right to demonstrate, including legislation that enabled a state of emergency to be called, were passed. While the Social Democrats continued to attract the most votes of any party in Vienna, they saw their overall electoral majority gradually disappear as power shifted in 1930 towards the conservatives.

As the Depression deepened across Europe, unemployment in Austria rose to 25 per cent. In 1930, the Christian Social Party assumed power under Engelbert Dollfuss as chancellor. A conservative with democratic leanings, he endeavoured to curtail anti-Semitism by outlawing discrimination against Jews in housing and jobs and invited the Social Democrats to join a broad coalition to address the country's dire economic situation. Historical outcomes might have been different had the Social Democrats accepted. However, they were reluctant, fearing that cooperation with Dollfuss would split the party and alienate many of its supporters. Thus rejected, Dollfuss turned instead to the political right, in particular, the Catholic Church, and opportunity for a broader-based coalition was lost.

On Hitler's assumption of power in Germany in January 1933, Austria's small Nazi Party craved for a similar triumph at home and began experimenting with a politics of terror. Their most effective tactic was to plant bombs in places frequented by tourists, since tourism was Austria's most lucrative industry. Dollfuss reacted by prohibiting the Nazi uniform to be worn in public, which was countered by Nazis parading shirtless. The tit for tat continued as Dollfuss instituted a ban on the Nazi Party, to which Hitler responded by imposing a visa charge on all Germans travelling to Austria, thus at a stroke reducing by 30 per cent Austria's income from tourism.

Following clashes and counterdemonstrations, Dollfuss outlawed Austria's small Communist Party, as well as the Schutzbund, the paramilitary wing of the Social Democratic Party, forcing both underground along with the Nazi Party. All opposition thus vanquished, Dollfuss set about creating a new, one-party grouping called the Vaterländische (Fatherland) Front aimed at re-establishing Austria as Europe's Christian-German bulwark against both Nazism and communism. Adopting a version of Mussolini's economics, Dollfuss announced plans to organise Austria constitutionally as a Catholic, ethnically German, corporatist state governed by a single united political party.

Though overtly unifying in intention, the outcome was immediate and divisive. The Social Democratic Party and now outlawed Schutzbund this time took to the streets. Though eventually crushed, the uprising resulted in more than fifteen hundred deaths, five thousand injuries, and over a thousand imprisoned. Most of the Social Democrats leadership escaped, but eleven Schutzbunders were caught, tried, and hanged. This left the nation in shock and further weakened the Social Democrats' and wider political opposition's capacity to confront and obstruct the rise of Nazism.

Following the failure of the uprising, Chancellor Dollfuss's powers were further extended. Any claim to a reinstatement of stability, however, was short-lived. Another revolt in July 1934, this time by Austrian Nazis, though again unsuccessful resulted in the death of Dollfuss himself. His replacement, Kurt von Schuschnigg, survived as chancellor for four years. In 1938, under considerable pressure from Austrian and German Nazis, Schuschnigg announced that a plebiscite (referendum) would take place on whether Austria should be joined to Germany. The expectation was that the Austrian electorate would vote for independence. However, the result was pre-empted by the Austrian Nazi Party which forcibly entered government on 11 March, immediately cancelling the plebiscite. German troops crossed the Austrian border a day later, and Schuschnigg was deposed and imprisoned. A Nazi frontman, Arthur Seyss-Inquart, was appointed in his place. His first task was to draft legislation to reduce Austria to a province of Germany, signing it into law on 13 March.

Hitler's tanks rolled across the border to a rapturous welcome of what seemed like the entire Austrian population. It is perhaps not surprising, given the continuing high level of unemployment and number of recent revolts and uprisings. Austrians found attractive Hitler's promise of strong leadership, full employment, and greater prosperity. For the Jewish minority, however, Hitler's presence marked the end of emancipation, freedom, prosperity, and a secure future. I have no knowledge of what happened on that day to the Dinger family or how they felt. Contemporary accounts give a sense of the dread felt by many Viennese Jews. Take, for example, the response of fifteen-year-old George Clare as he walked home from his grandmother's house:

> I walked home. I had gone about halfway, when the first squadron of German bombers appeared over Vienna. Flying in exact formation and very low, they looked big and black against the blue sky, their engines throbbing menacingly. Squadron followed upon squadron, more and more Luftwaffe planes, hundreds and hundreds of them, circled the city. I can only repeat, in describing the scene, the cliché of the plane-blackened sky, because it is literally true. All they dropped on Vienna were propaganda leaflets, but I could not help thinking, as I watched them, of my talk with…my other school friends only the afternoon before and how determined we had been to fight the Nazis. What chance would we have against this mighty air force? How much of Vienna would be standing now had they dropped bombs instead of bits of paper?[43]

Similarly, the Dingers' initial emotions must have been fear and uncertainly. What would happen? Could they get out? If so, how, when, and where? Or should they just sit tight and wait for the Austrians' frenzied love affair with Nazism to blow over?

Hope soon evaporated. It seemed that *the* most popular aspect of the Nazi presence was anti-Semitism. While only a minority of the mob were committed card-carrying Nazis, hatred of Jews, hitherto mostly acknowledged in private, was now out in the open. Vienna's first Jewish round-up came late in the afternoon of 12 March. As Clare describes 'Jews, business men and professionals, women and children, the old and sick as well as the young and healthy, were rounded up and forced to do menial and debasing work out in the streets, surrounded by a cheering and laughing mob.'[44]

This public expression of hostility to ordinary Jews – not the Nazi stereotyped plutocrats or Orthodox Jews – was particularly shocking to my mother and was one of the few incidents of her former life that she spoke of to me. An evening of frenzied joy followed with column upon column of jubilant Viennese marching towards the city centre. Hitler himself arrived in Linz, where he had lived as a child. The hysterical nature of his welcome persuaded him of the likely acceptance by the Austrians of the full incorporation of Austria into the German Reich – Anschluss – rather than deployment of German troops as an occupying force. The enthusiasm displayed towards Hitler and the Germans surprised Nazis and non-Nazis alike. Hitler's procession through Austria became a triumphant tour that came to a climax on 15 March, when two hundred thousand Austrians crushed into the Heldenplatz (Square of Heroes) in Vienna to listen to Hitler announcing the unification of the two countries.

The Anschluss had disastrous consequences for the Jewish community and all in it, regardless of whether they were rich or poor, Orthodox or secular, Yiddish- or German-speaking, westernised or from the East. The new Austrian regime immediately sought to impose similar laws and restrictions as those in the 'Fatherland', known as the Nuremberg Laws. Tens of thousands of men and women, primarily political opponents and Jews, were arrested, and the first deportations to Dachau took place within a month. A rigged plebiscite in April resulted in near unanimous support for the incorporation of Austria into Germany – Jews by then had been stripped of all their citizen's rights and were not allowed to vote. The persecution of Jews and anyone who dared to express opposition to the Nazi regime also started immediately. Due to an 'Anschluss from the inside', the Nuremberg Laws were speedier and more effectively imposed in Austria than in Germany. Austrian Nazis and their followers matched the invasion by rushing, first to humiliate the Jews and then to persecute them 'in the most brutal, bestialized manner'.[45]

One remembered story from my mother was how Jews, when outside, could be forced by Nazi officials to get down on their knees and scrub the pavements.

The predominant feeling among Jewish families was shock – that things had happened so quickly and that they had not predicted so swift a rise of Nazism in Austria. Shock followed upon shock as their civic status was eroded and as they lost their jobs, professions, livelihoods, homes, possessions, and some their lives. No protection could be expected from the police or military. Nor was there much sympathy from non-Jewish teachers, school friends, or neighbours, though, it must be said, some remained steadfast. But there were only a few individuals and groups – of Social Democrats, Catholics, and Christian Social Party members – who were brave enough to express their sadness, anger, and shame at what was happening.

As the Viennese Jewish population faced the destruction of their worlds, the women and the young seemed better able to cope than were the men and the old. While the men tended to look backwards with sadness and helplessness, the women looked forward to finding a way out of their predicament. The older Dinger sisters, for example, sought to re-establish contact with their first cousins in London, while Tilda made contact with her husband's relatives on the East Coast of the United States of America. An unexpected bonus of Vienna's outburst of popular anti-Semitism and its speed and intensity was that hitherto doubtful members of the Jewish population immediately started taking steps to leave, and as a result, many thousands of Jewish lives were saved. The heightened levels of anti-Semitism also created a stronger awareness of and pride in being Jewish and a spirit of ingenuity and defiance in challenging the lengthening odds. In contrast to Germany, where many opted to continue to live under Nazi rule in the belief that ordinary Germans would come to their senses, the extremeness of the Austrian response to the Anschluss left no one in any doubt about what would happen if they stayed.

Kristallnacht proved the final straw. On the night of 9 November 1938, Nazi paramilitary forces and civilians carried out a series of coordinated attacks on Jewish property throughout Nazi Germany and Austria, undeterred and unchallenged by official authorities. The name Kristallnacht or Night of the Broken Glass comes from the shards of broken glass that littered the streets, fragments from the smashed windows of synagogues and Jewish-owned shops, homes, and community buildings. More recently, Kristallnacht is more commonly seen by historians of Nazism in Germany, not as a night of glittering glass, but as a devastating and degrading pogrom. For example, Walter E. Pehle argues that using the word Kristallnacht in fact minimises the actuality of manslaughter, murder, arson, robbery, plunder, and massive property damage that occurred. [46] Virtually all the synagogues in Vienna and throughout other German-occupied and controlled territories were vandalised and destroyed on that one night, tens of thousands of Jews were injured, dozens were killed, and a ruinous tax was imposed on the entire Jewish population.[47]

With the family shoe shop scheduled for 'Aryanisation', a term coined for the forced expulsion of so-called 'non-Aryans', mainly Jews, from business life in Nazi Germany and the territories it controlled[48] and work opportunities disappearing fast, Steffi and her siblings made immediate preparations for escape. So indeed did almost the entire Jewish community. Consequently, half the Viennese Jewish population managed to escape before borders were closed. Living in the capital made it easier for them to get hold of the relevant travel documents than those living in rural areas, and city dwellers had fewer difficulties getting together paperwork and finding payment for the range of leaving taxes demanded by the Nazi authorities.

The Nazi authorities, at this time, were largely concerned with financial considerations and property ownership. For example, Jewish adults were obliged, by the cut-off date of 27 April 1938, to complete a form indicating their monthly income (133.33 schillings in Steffi's case)[49], plus details of bank accounts, possessions, and valuables. Among the possessions listed by Steffi were two bracelets valued at 100 schillings, three rings (45 sch.), one brooch (35 sch.), one necklace (30 sch.), two pairs of earrings (50 sch.) and one watch (30 sch.) – 290 schillings in all. [50] How much of this she was able to take out of the country I do not know, though she certainly managed to retain some small bits of jewellery for her arrival in London. Many, however, were careful not to disclose the entirety of their possessions, in the certainty that they would need to draw on financial resources to pay for their way out.

Opportunities for corruption were rife, with bureaucrats willing to accept bribes in exchange for easing the process of departure. One can only speculate on what the Dinger sisters had to do to acquire the correct exit documentation. No doubt, where young women were concerned, sexual favours of some sort were part and parcel of the negotiation. Bank accounts were emptied and jewellery pawned. Adolf Eichmann, a major architect of the Holocaust, was at this time working in Vienna, where he used his considerable organisational talents to get the largest number of Jews out of the country in the shortest period of time, while at the same time exacting from them the greatest amount of wealth and property possible.

Steffi's visa application was dated July 1938, and new German passports were issued to Steffi and her younger sisters, Elsa and Trude, in October 1938.[51] The three sisters eventually left for Britain in December 1938 (Steffi and Elsa) and January 1939 (Trude). Getting the appropriate documents together to get permission to leave Austria was an undoubted triumph, yet it did not guarantee entry into Britain.

Early in 1938, an estimated ten thousand Jewish refugees were in the United Kingdom. The government showed little interest in imposing restrictions on their entry, since it was felt that the benefits these new arrivals brought with them substantially outweighed any potential disadvantages.[52] However, this position came to an abrupt end on German's annexation of Austria, which resulted in a dramatic increase in applications from migrants with Austrian passports. Parliament and the government reacted, perhaps predictably, by enforcing restrictions to entry. In rejecting a proposal for the Home Office to have increased powers to admit Austrian refugees, Samuel Hoare, then Home Secretary, explained that, while he was sympathetic to applications from refugees able to work in the sciences, arts, business, and industry, whose presence would be advantageous to Britain, other applications would be treated less favourably. *Usefulness*, rather than need of refuge or risk from persecution, was the watchword. This inevitably discriminated against the poor, unskilled, very young, and very old.

Other countries followed suit. For example, Czechoslovakia sealed its borders against Jewish refugees from Austria within hours of the Anschluss in 1938. The Belgian statesman Paul-Henri Spaak, previously celebrated for his liberalism, announced that there could be no wholesale immigration of foreigners into Belgium, and US Secretary of State Cordell Hull made it clear that no increase in German or Austrian immigration could be contemplated. Unemployment, trade union opposition to foreign labour, and threat of igniting dangerous waves of anti-Semitism were the most frequently cited excuses for keeping the Jews out.

Thus, just as Steffi and her sisters successfully negotiated their exit from Vienna and began to seek refuge in Britain, Britain was introducing various measures to keep them out. Two kinds of entry visa were available to them. The first, for those categorised as political refugees, allowed residence for three months only, with a requirement to register with police and not do paid work. The second was for workers predicted to fill gaps in the labour market. After October 1938, the Home Office took over responsibility for processing applications, denoting a change in admissions policy. The officials that once welcomed migrants who could help meet labour market needs were now concerned with keeping them out, on grounds of security and effective immigration management. More checks were introduced. For example, prospective employers in Britain were carefully scrutinised by the (voluntary) Jewish Coordinating Committee, while on the Austrian side, processing employment visas was shared between the Viennese Jewish Community (Israelitische Kultusgemeinde) and the Society of Friends (Quakers), which had an office in Vienna. The policy favoured young women, since the highest demand for labour was for female domestic servants.

Steffi's application provides an illuminating example of how the procedures worked. According to her Home Office file, her application was initially successful because she was guaranteed domestic employment (by her cousin Fanny) and had practical experience in leather glove making and weaving – all assumed to be of potential value to the British economy.[53] So even though she entered Britain on a so-called domestic visa, Steffi's potential contribution to other areas of work was taken into account in the decision on whether to allow entry.

As 1938 came to an end and the intentions of the Nazis became clearer, panic set in within the Austrian Jewish community, more so after Kristallnacht in November. In Vienna, as in other Austrian cities, every means was sought to gain the necessary papers for departure, every avenue explored, every contact contacted. Organisations responsible for processing Austrian refugees were overwhelmed by the complex procedures introduced by the Nazis and by distraught individuals and family groups waiting in line often for days on end to get seen. Queuing was particularly hazardous, leaving people vulnerable to the whims of passing Nazi officers, who might at any time order individuals to undertake a work detail, or to the prejudices of officials, who were often deliberately obstructive. As George Clare remembers:

> After queuing for hours at the constant risk of being hijacked from the queue by a passing SS patrol for a few hours of cleaning their barracks, you finally faced the official that you had come to see. In eight cases out of ten you had done it all wrong. [Then it was] back to the starting point to get a chit to another office to get a chit from another official entitling you to talk to the first one. And when you had come back, duly equipped with the right piece of paper, after queuing for another few hours, then this stamp was not right or that document wrong and you started all

over again. The inventiveness of Nazi officials knew
no bounds.[54]

Vienna became a notorious bottleneck. Complaints about delays,
rudeness and discouragement flooded into the Foreign Office in
London, from refugee organisations, public figures, and indignant
non-refugee travellers. It is a wonder that the three ordinary Dinger
sisters, with little influence or money, succeeded in cutting through
the red tape, negotiating the numerous bureaucratic pitfalls, and
getting out of Austria and into Britain.

The British authorities would not countenance applications
without a named guarantor who was willing to promise that no
financial demands would be incurred by the state. The Dinger sisters
were fortunate in having such a person to vouch for them. We have
already seen that Fanny had visited the Dinger household in Vienna
a decade or more earlier, in 1927, when she and Steffi had developed a
special bond. As we have also seen, Fanny and Steffi were of a similar
age. Both were outgoing, strong-willed, and independent, and it is
probably these characteristics that created a mutual trust and affection
that lasted a lifetime. It was individuals as well as organisations that
made escape possible. And so it was that the Dinger sisters found
themselves in London just as war was breaking out.

CHAPTER 6

Amalia in Vienna, 1900–1942

I now return to the first decades of the twentieth century in Vienna, where Amalia, following her departure from Brody, spent most of the rest of her life and where she gave birth to Gisela (my namesake), Steffi, and her other children. Vienna was as different from her hometown as London is to one of the outposts of the British Empire – when Britain had an empire, that is! In making the move to Vienna, Amalia was taking a huge step into the unknown. Other members of the family sought to escape the restrictive and impoverished conditions in Brody and moved elsewhere – to Britain (London) and probably to the United States or perhaps South America. In 1899, Amalia set out for life in Vienna with her prospective husband, David Hirsch, primarily to seek out a better life.

It is likely that they went through a Jewish marriage ceremony before they left Brody for Vienna. Otherwise, one imagines, their respective (and respectable) families would not have allowed them to leave. For Jews from Eastern Europe at the time, the West (and that included Vienna) signified the opportunity to live a better life with greater freedom and more possibilities of work. They had learnt, from engineers travelling from the West, about new technologies and inventions and, from traders and travellers, about new ideas in books and literature and, from travelling artists and musicians, about Western trends in fashion and culture. All of this evoked a *modern* world, which must have seemed inescapably glamorous and enticing. They did not anticipate the blackened factory chimneys; the squalor; and, as Roth describes, the 'sheer hatred' that they would meet when they got to the West.

There is no record of Amalia's arrival in Vienna. Nor do we have anything to tell us with whom she travelled. We do know that she would have come by train, first to L'viv, the main town in the region of Galicia, and then via Krakow to Vienna. There may have been relatives already in Vienna waiting to welcome her who had already arranged accommodation and work possibilities. Or David may have gone on ahead to oversee such arrangements. Amalia's younger unmarried sister, Frieda, would have accompanied her, particularly as Amalia was in the early stages of her first pregnancy. One can only imagine how exciting it must have been for all of them to leave their provincial home town for the bright lights of Vienna. From an invitation (see below) sent to her brother Sigmund Dinger in L'viv, we know that Amalia took part in an official marriage ceremony with David Hirsch at the main synagogue in Vienna on 3 September 1899. She was twenty-five.

The ceremony gave legitimacy to the couple's first child, Malvine, born some six months later. From my mother, I learnt that Amalia and David were first cousins. Marriage within the family was more common in those days because families were much larger; a family of ten children or more was not unusual. As a consequence, most socialising took place within the family and immediate relations, at occasions marking religious festivals as well as births, marriages, and deaths. So falling in love with the daughter or son of an uncle or aunt on such an occasion was common and accepted – and at least there would be no doubt about the suitability and background of any suitor.

Curiously, the names of the wedding couple on the invitation are Amalia Dinger and David Hirsch, so it might have been expected that the future family name would be Hirsch, derived from the bridegroom. Why Dinger, rather than Hirsch, became the family name is not clear. The name Moszkowicz appears (on Amalia's children's birth certificates), so we can assume that this was Amalia's mother's family name. From the Jewish Records Office in Vienna, we can see that several graves in Brody's Jewish Cemetery bear the name of Moscizker or Moshtzisker and many more, the name Hirsch, including several rabbis. Perhaps, then, Hirsch was a prosperous branch of the family with business connections in Vienna. Less common is a nineteenth-century grave in Brody with the name Dinger. It could be that the Dinger part of the family originated from elsewhere. The only people with Dinger as their family name listed on Yad Vashem's database of Shoah victims, apart from Amalia and Frieda, are three from Odessa (Nina, born 1869; Anna, born 1901; and Basya, born 1891) plus a Hermann Dinger from Merseburg in Saxony. Odessa lies in the south of present-day Ukraine on the Black Sea and may have been the place where a branch of Amalia's family known as Dinger originated. There is a long history of movement between Brody and Odessa, and indeed, Galician and German Jews in Odessa were styled 'Broder' Jews after the city of Brody and were particularly influential in the nineteenth century.[55] Nina, three years older than Amalia, could well have been a distant cousin.

Another explanation for keeping the mother's name was that, in Brody, most wedding ceremonies were religious rather than official. Therefore any offspring, considered formally illegitimate by the authorities, would be expected to take their mother's, rather than their father's, name. Or Amalia and David may have adopted Dinger as a family name because it sounds less Jewish, in line with many other Jews who altered their names to fit more easily into their newly adopted countries and cultures. But these are mere speculations, and it is unlikely that we shall ever know for certain.

We find that, when Amalia arrived in Vienna in 1899, David Hirsch was already living there because Nestrogasse, 4/3 is the address on the wedding invitation (above) to which people are asked to reply. It is likely that the couple would have already been living together there because Amalia was already David's wife in the eyes of her family and the Jewish community, if not the state. As noted, Amalia's sister Frieda could have made the initial journey with her (with or without David) or arrived in time for the official wedding ceremony. She could have, perhaps, arrived even later, say on the birth of Amalia's first or second child.

Several other addresses are given for the family Dinger in Vienna. The young couple had two children at their first apartment. Malvine was born 9 February 1900. She died in childhood, and no record exists of the date of her death. Gisela, after whom I was named, was born 18 July 1901.

Amalia and David would later move to a more convenient apartment in Föstergasse behind the shoe shop. This apartment was leased by Sigmund Dinger, Amalia's brother, and managed by David. The family lived there for over twenty years, and there Steffi and her younger sisters and brothers were born. Both of the Dinger apartments were damaged in the 1939–45 war and the blocks rebuilt, so it is difficult to ascertain with any certainty the living conditions then or the reasons for the couple's next and final move.

This was in 1924 to flat two, 12 Krummbaumgasse, a large apartment in a newer building, located in what was clearly a more prosperous part of Leopoldstadt. Situated along one side of Carmelite Market square, the original building still stands– a tall multi-storey building with an impressively large front door and long winding staircase. On one of my visits to Vienna, I managed to get into the building but, unfortunately, not into apartment 12 where the Dingers lived. It was from Krummbaumgasse that different members of the family departed from Vienna for the last time.

All three homes were in Vienna's second district, historically a Jewish area known as Leopoldstadt, and perhaps the eventual destination also of other relations or neighbours from Brody.

When David and Amalia arrived in 1899, Vienna was at the peak of its influence as capital of the massive, multicultural Austro-Hungarian Empire, even if in its final years of full prosperity. Franz Joseph I was Emperor of Austria as well as King of Bohemia, Croatia, and Hungary. He had come to the throne in 1848, aged eighteen years, and was to remain there until his death in 1916, one of the longest serving monarchs in Europe. At the time the young couple was settling in, Franz Joseph had been emperor for more than half a century and had transformed Vienna from an old medieval city into a modern metropolis with a great arc of imperial buildings, including a city hall, the Austrian Parliament Building, an opera house, a museum district, and a university. The new Ring Road (Ringstrasse), edged by palaces and other ornamental residences of the rich and powerful, faced away from the old city wall and towards what was then perceived as a politically, culturally, and architecturally magnificent future. Its completion took decades of building, and for many years, Vienna must have been an enormous building site. But by the time Amalia and David arrived, the buildings, parks, and open spaces were all complete and in place, and the two were no doubt much in awe as they viewed the huge neoclassical buildings and marble statuary – all so different from small-town Brody.

Jews were prominent in the rebuilding of Vienna, with a number of palaces and grand buildings along the Ringstrasse built and inhabited by recently wealthy Jewish families, for instance, the

Ephrussi brothers, originally from Odessa in Russia. However, most Jews lived in the poorer parts of the city, such as Leopoldstadt. 'Go to the slums of Vienna, Leopoldstadt,' De Waal writes, 'and you can see Jews living as Jews should live, twelve in a room, no water, loud on the street, wearing the right robes, speaking the right argot.'[56]

Jews had cause to be grateful to Emperor Franz Josef because of his removal of the last barriers to their full citizenship in 1867; in particular, they were now able to own property. This was important for the revival of Vienna, since Jewish families made rich by trade but restricted by law from buying land, owning property, and engaging in professions could now invest in the rebuilding of the city. Following the pull factors of the actions of Franz Josef and greater cultural and religious freedom offered by Vienna and the push factors of pogroms and persecution elsewhere, Jews moved to the city in increasing numbers. The Jewish community expanded, from 6,217 in 1857 (2 per cent of the population) to 72,000 in 1880 (10 per cent of the population). By the turn of the twentieth century, there were 100,000 Jews in Vienna, mostly living in or near Leopoldstadt. The flow from East to West continued, from Galicia, Bohemia, Moravia, and Hungary, with many of the incomers initially continuing their home practices of speaking Yiddish, wearing robes rather than modern dress, and observing religious traditions and ceremonies.

At the time of Amalia and David's arrival in Vienna, a second and even third generation of Jews – the children of parents who had made the break with the East some three of four decades earlier – was beginning to flex its intellectual (and secular) muscles. This younger generation of Jews came into prominence in the city in different areas of public and civic life – banking, theatre, literature, law, medicine, journalism, and so on. They were *modern* Viennese citizens who, while still mainly identifying as Jews although some converted to Christianity, adopted and absorbed the more sophisticated habits of the West. They spoke the national language and read the national literature (both German) and adopted modern behaviour, dress, and culture. They celebrated their freedom by achieving hitherto unimaginable things. Glittering Jewish Viennese of this period included the composers Gustav Mahler and Arnold Schönberg; the writers Stefan Zweig, Joseph Roth and Karl Kraus; and psychoanalysts such as Sigmund Freud and Alfred Adler, as well as numerous Jewish scientists and doctors, many Nobel Prize winners included.

By the turn of the twentieth century, Vienna had fifty-nine synagogues of various denominations, as well as a wide network of elementary and secondary Jewish schools. By 1923, the Viennese Jewish community was the third largest in Europe and had reached the high point of its influence. However, just as the Viennese Jewish community, rich and poor, reached ever-dizzying heights, the roots of its eventual destruction were already visible.

The great Austro-Hungarian Empire, which had provided them with space to breathe and prosper, was on the losing side in the First World War. Following the Treaty of Versailles, Vienna was now an overblown but lively capital of a much-reduced Austria with a population of only six million. Anti-Semitism, which had been given added oxygen before the war in the populist rhetoric of mayor Karl Lueger, continued to exert its ugly attraction at the end of the war to a young Austrian corporal, Adolf Hitler, now demobbed and unemployed. It was relatively easy for Hitler and others to find a scapegoat for their nation's loss of power, prestige, and empire. The discourse was familiar and the arguments ready-made – it was primarily the fault of the Jews. And so a terrible era for the world began to take shape, out of the ashes of empire and grandeur.

But let us return to Amalia and David and their wedding in 1899 in the central Viennese synagogue. There is no photograph remaining of the wedding, but I imagine that it would have been a modern ceremony, with at least some guests in Western garb. It was likely to have been a small wedding, as there had already been an outlay for the religious ceremony in Brody. Moreover, the cost of train tickets for the extended Brody family to Vienna would have been high. Amalia's older brother, Sigmund, was no doubt at the ceremony, his photographs suggesting someone comfortable with travelling long distances across the empire. Frieda, as we have already surmised, may have been present, having accompanied her older sister on the long journey from Brody. She perhaps agreed to live with the newlyweds at least until she could find a job and/or husband for herself. It is doubtful whether Amalia's parents could afford to attend, but perhaps members of the more prosperous Hirsch family on the bridegroom's side might have been better represented.

Vienna's second district, Leopoldstadt, where the couple lived, was named after Holy Roman Emperor Leopold I, who forcibly evicted the small Jewish community in the seventeenth century. It is situated on a large island surrounded by the Danube Canal with the Danube River to the north. Nearby is the Wiener Prater, formerly imperial hunting grounds and, for more than a century, a large amusement park, known as the Volksprater ('People's Prater'). At its entrance is the giant Ferris wheel opened in 1897, which featured prominently in the film *The Third Man*. Originally on the site of the old ghetto, migrant Jews settled in Leopoldstadt, due primarily to its proximity to the Nordbahnhof (railway station), one of the main entry points into the city from different parts of the empire. So many Jews lived there that the area became known as Mazzesinsel ('Matzo Island') after matzo, a type of unleavened bread eaten during the Jewish Passover festival. It was also home of the famed Vienna Boys' Choir.

The family Dinger continued to expand; nine children were born between 1900 and 1917, with a large gap before Trude's birth in 1917. The Jewish Records Office provides an explanation for this gap; two children were born between Tilda and Trude – Hedwig on 9 October 1910 and Karl on 14 January 1914, both of whom died in infancy.

After the war ended, conditions began to improve, though we do not know how the family sustained itself for the decade following. David Dinger took over running a shoe shop sometime during that period, while his wife and sister-in-law looked after the children and managed the household. Photographs suggest that the family gradually became more prosperous. All the children extended their education beyond compulsory school. For example, Steffi and Trude both attended secretarial college, which included tuition in one or two foreign languages. Among Trude's belongings are certificates showing her assessed competence in spoken French and English.

Advertised as a 'superior' shoe shop selling 'luxury' shoes at the cheapest of prices (see the photograph of Frieda with the shop in the background below), the enterprise was presumably successful because, in 1924, the family could afford to move to a larger apartment. The pictures below denote two contrasting aspects of Amalia's family in Vienna. The picture of Sigmund, her older brother, is a studio portrait, showing him as jaunty, prosperous, and clearly a man about town. He was a businessman and commercial traveller who plied his trade across the Empire. The picture of Frieda, sister of Sigmund and Amalia, is more of a family snap taken outside the shop. She appears homelier and less concerned about clothes and appearance. As an unmarried woman living in her sister's family home, she was much more limited to the private and domestic sphere, with her time divided between helping raise the family, organising the household, and serving in the family business.

Public and private, business and domesticity were all part and parcel of what it meant to be a modern family in Vienna in the 1920s – gendered certainly as far as the older generation was concerned, but less so perhaps for the children.

This period was arguably the highpoint of Amalia's life. She and her husband had successfully integrated into (Jewish) Viennese life; they had a flourishing shoe shop; and their children were growing up strong, confident, and educated.

Disaster struck in 1928 when David died suddenly of a heart attack while out of town. However, Amalia was able to transfer the lease of the flat into her own name (we have already seen that Sigmund's name was on the shop lease), and life went on. The older children were by now working. Steffi was employed from 1928 as a clerk and later as administrator in a series of local businesses; Elsa was a shop assistant; and Trude, the youngest child, when she was old enough, became a clerk like Steffi. The remaining sisters in all probability did the same, although we have no record of if and where they worked. Their brother Moritz may have gone into commerce of some sort, perhaps with an extended family member. Or perhaps, like his sisters, he went into office or retail work. In family photographs, he appears 'white collared' and well dressed, as pictured below with Steffi and a very young Trude. He was fondly remembered by his sisters, with no evident reputation either as entrepreneur or ne'er-do-well. So it is likely that he had a modest job that enabled him to contribute to the family income.

Amalia, we must assume, spent most of the 1920s and 1930s in the home, looking after her large family and assisting David in the shoe shop, aided by Frieda. However, for her children, Vienna was a cultural and artistic playground. The 1920s was a vibrant decade in the city, particularly for the young. The new post-war social democratic government was instituting major and internationally acclaimed reforms in housing and social policy, which extended well into the 1930s. The coffee houses, cinemas, theatres, and opera were all available to the young Dingers with a little money jingling in their pockets. Amalia must have been so proud to see her modern Viennese family prospering in the new modern Austria.

In describing his own life in the 1920s in Vienna, the historian Eric Hobsbawm wrote that 'for Jews to be "German" was not a political or national but a cultural project'. It meant creating a distance between 'the backwardness of the shtetls and shuls [synagogues and prayer houses]' and joining the modern world. They wanted to speak German rather than Yiddish because they aspired to be German rather than emulate their more religious Eastern cousins, that is, 'the Hasidim with their miracle-working hereditary *wunderrabbis* or the *yeshiva-bokhers* explicating the Talmud in Yiddish'[57]. Like Eric Hobsbawm's relatives, Amalia and her family had little idea about the dangers that threatened them. They were always aware of anti-Semitism, and indeed the Christian Social Party in the 1920s remained as anti-Semitic as its founder, Mayor Lueger. However, they were shocked when news came of the 1930 German Reichstag election in which Hitler's National Socialists became the second largest party and horrified when they took control in Germany in 1933. In these circumstances, it was impossible for Amalia and her family to forget that they were Jews, however emancipated and modern.

Hobsbawm claims that the different generations of Jews were divided about how to deal with the rising threat of state-sponsored anti-Semitism. The older generation advocated keeping a low profile, staying on the right side of the law, and taking evasive action only when necessary – presumably this was Amalia's stance as she approached her sixties. Her children, however, were more defiant. Active as Social Democrats, they called for resistance and an end to prejudice and injustice. However, neither generation could anticipate that the political goal of Nazism was their annihilation. Otherwise, they may have acted more swiftly to leave.

The end of the 1920s and early 1930s were marked by increasing political conflict between left and right, against a backdrop of prolonged social and economic crisis and Depression, as we have already seen. Violent attacks on Jews and others increased following Dollfuss' death in 1934. His successor Kurt Schusschnigg attempted to find a compromise with Hitler without loss of Austria's sovereignty but failed. The unopposed entry of the German army on 12 March 1938 marked the definitive end of the Austrian 'mini-state'. Not a shot was fired. Welcomed by 'hysterically cheering crowds',[58] Hitler made the last visit he was ever to make to Austria, the country of his birth.

While the Dinger family cannot have predicted the eventual terrible outcome of Nazi persecution of the Jews, they were more fortunate than others, in the sense that, while not wealthy, they were living in the capital city and had relatives abroad who could vouch for them. They were thus in a position to manage the bureaucracy of visas, passports, and other documentation necessary for emigration. There was a rush to escape, but only four of the children managed it, and none of the older generation. Steffi, Elsa, and Trude travelled individually at different times to London and settled there. Moritz, Amalia's only son, fled to Riga in Latvia. A photograph of him there dated 20 April 1939 gives an impression of order and safety.

Moritz was certainly safe in the short term, but eventually the war extended to the Baltic States (Estonia, Latvia, and Lithuania), when in 1940, they were occupied by the Soviet Union as a result of the Soviet–Nazi pact. Soviet rule was short-lived however, and within weeks of the ending of the pact, the German Army invaded the Baltic territories and, following this, incorporated them, like Austria, into the Third Reich. We do not know how Moritz survived between 1939 and 1944 when the Soviet Union Army again marched in as the Germans retreated. As an Austrian Jewish exile, living first under the Russians and then under the Nazis, conditions could not have been easy. Moritz must have had luck or skill or both to overcome the multiple difficulties he faced in just keeping alive. However, eventually his fate was sealed when he was picked up in 1944 by the Soviet secret police, designated a German-speaking enemy alien, and transported to a work camp, Karaganda (Karlag), now in Kazakhstan. There, he eventually died – in 1945, just as the war was ending.

Karlag was another of the horrors emerging from this dismal period of human history. It was one of the largest of fifty or more 'corrective' labour camps established in the Soviet Union. Unlike other Soviet labour camps, which focused on mining or construction, Karlag was an agricultural camp. Established in September 1931 during Stalin's 'collectivisation' period, the aim was to turn the barren steppe into fertile fields for crops and grazing. To this end, sub-camps were spread across a great distance. By the start of the war in 1939, such camps contained around 1.3 million largely political prisoners.[59] Writing about her own experience in Karlag between 1939 and 1941, Margaret Buber-Neumann records that she could gain no sense of the camp's size because it was so large; indeed, it covered an area equivalent to the size of Denmark or the Netherlands.[60] She writes that prisoners faced appalling conditions with filth, hunger, and disease rampant and shortages of everything. Although death rates were high during Buber-Neumann's stay, they rose even more after war broke out between the Soviet Union and Germany in 1941. In an already weakened state after his wartime stay in Riga and his transport eastwards, Moritz could not survive the conditions at Karlag and died only a few months after his arrival.

His younger sister, Tilda, was more successful in her attempts at escape, although initially her future also looked bleak. Steffi's second youngest sister had married in 1935 and borne a son, George. It was more difficult for her to gain exit documents for both of them, so she remained in Vienna after the rest had left. Her husband, Max Bertish, was stranded for the duration of the war in Switzerland. Left to her own devices, she moved back to the family home in the hope that an opportunity to escape would present itself. That moment came early in 1941. Scheduled for deportation to a work/death camp, Tilda had no choice but to run. She raided what was left of the family coffers to purchase tickets for one of the last few trains going eastwards – at the same time as Russian soldiers were heading west. Austria's western borders were already closed due to the war in Europe, so any escape in that direction was impossible. Tilda and George caught the train westwards through Poland, passing work and death camps along the way (where, according to George, the carriage curtains were drawn) and entered Russia. Here, they changed trains due to a difference in the rail gauge size in Russia. George remembers that they remained on the Trans-Siberian Railway for more than a week, eventually arriving in Shanghai where, precocious for his age (he says that), he helped guide his mother across the city to catch the steamer to Yokohama in Japan. From Yokohama, they took yet another steamer to Seattle, arriving just before the United States entered the war and the ports were sealed. Thereafter, they travelled across the American continent, finally reaching Tilda's husband's relatives in Newark. This epic journey – the huge obstacles placed before the travellers and how they were surmounted – can only be imagined. But it did happen. Tilda and George reached safety and lived to tell the tale. Finally reunited with her husband, Max, after the war, Tilda and her family remained and settled in Newark. Theirs was a truly remarkable story and an astounding escape.

Things did not go as well for Gisela, the oldest of the Dinger siblings. Like her brother and sisters, she applied for an exit visa. An emigration questionnaire signed by Gisela Dinger and dated 15 May 1938, sought permission to leave Austria together with her mother, Malke Dinger, and her aunt, Frieda Moszkowicz.[61] Though an entry in the questionnaire indicated that London was the preferred destination, other possible alternatives included North America and Australia. The main address given in London was Fanny Isenstein's house in London, so we must suppose that Steffi and her other siblings filled out similar questionnaires at this time. Gisela's application was unsuccessful, and she was not granted a visa. She remained at home with her mother and aunt and also latterly with Tilda and George. However, she was not to witness Tilda's departure to the United States of American. Nor did she share the fate of her mother and aunt. Whether or not due to the anxieties of living through such a stressful period, Gisela was diagnosed with ovarian cancer and died on 2 February 1940 at the age of only thirty-eight. She was buried near the graves of her father, David, and Uncle Sigmund, in the Jewish section of the Viennese municipal cemetery. Only a few more Jewish burials were to take place after Gisela's death, as from 1942 onwards the Nazis turned to other ways of disposing of their Jewish dead.

Gisela's burial must have been heart-rending for Amalia. Her daughter's death certificate, affirmed by Amalia's shaky signature, lists her children as mainly abroad – three in London, one in Riga, and only only one (Tilda) living at home (see below). Notable is the second name of Malke Dinger's signature. 'Sara' was enforced on all Jewish females by the Nazi regime. Similarly, Jewish men were forcibly designated 'Israel'.

It must have been an immense relief for Amalia to know that three of her daughters were safe in London, at least for the moment, and that her son was alive and well in Riga – even as she grieved her loss. She was distraught over the death of her eldest daughter, as were Gisela's London-based sisters, who received the news with shrieks and tears according to a young member of the London branch of the family. Amalia must have been anxious and eventually relieved when her remaining daughter, Tilda, and grandson, George, decided to leave for the United States. We can only hope that she received the good news that they had safely reached their destination of Newark.

By 1941, all Amalia's children and her only grandchild were gone. Amalia and her sister Frieda were left alone with no family or income; the shoe shop had been long ago handed over to non-Jews. Fortunately, they were allowed to stay in the Krummbaumgasse apartment. But that would not last for very long.

CHAPTER 7

Uszer in Belgium, 1923–1938

While the Social Democrats and then the Nazis were ruling Amalia and Steffi's lives, what had happened to Uszer on his arrival in Belgium and thereafter? The first glimpse we have of him in Belgium is in an official document from the Commune de Châtelineau dated 23 January 1923, announcing the arrival of Ensel Frucht. His date of birth is given as 1 January 1897, and his birthplace, Lodz, Poland. So Uszer first entered Belgium taking the name of Ensel with a Ukrainian passport, issued some four months before in Berlin on 2 September 1922.[62] Subsequent documents indicate that he arrived in Belgium from Alsdorf in North Rhine-Westphalia, near the border triangle of Germany, Belgium, and the Netherlands. He perhaps chose Alsdorf because it was a mining area where there was work to be had. Or possibly he went there because it offered an easy entry point into Belgium. He may have worked in Alsdorf for some months as Ensel's/Uszer's documentation mentions an identity card issued in Alsdorf on 12 September 1922, though there is no copy in his file. For whatever reason, in February 1923, Uszer took the decision to move to Belgium. He also decided to continue to use the name of Ensel, probably to protect himself from the attention of the Polish military authorities, who were after him as Uszer Frucht.

His application for residence was granted. For the next two years, he worked in the Bois du Cazier coal mines, until involved in an accident in which he lost half his thumb. Notorious as a dangerous place to work, the Bois du Cazier mine was the site of a serious mining accident in 1957, some twenty-five years after Uszer's time, when 262 miners, predominantly Italian migrants, died, with many lesser incidents before then. The coalfields had long been a magnet for migrants, as already noted, with the local Walloon (French-speaking) workforce favouring work in safer local industries, such as steel production. Seeking economic betterment, by 1930, French, Poles, Italians, and Czechs together constituted a fifth of the coalfield workforce.[63] While working there, Uszer regularly changed address, mostly moving between the neighbouring communes of Gilly, Marinelle, Charleroi, and Châtelineau. There is no indication of why he changed residence so often, but eventually he settled down in Charleroi with his prospective wife, Ruchla (or Rosa as she was known to her family) Demski and her family.

By 1927, Uszer had married Ruchla, of similar Polish origins to himself though from a somewhat wealthier family. They had two children, a son, Henri, and a daughter, Clara. Belgian family lore maintains that Uszer met his future wife at a performance of a local Jewish theatre group, and the 1924 photograph below certainly suggests a more sophisticated appearance than one might expect from an erstwhile miner. Having scrutinised the various passport-size photographs contained in Uszer's file, I can only conclude that Ensel and Uszer were indeed the same person and not, for instance, brothers. The tuft at the hairline seems a defining characteristic. The Belgian authorities reached the same conclusion, as we shall see later.

Uszer was invalided out on a small pension after the mining accident in 1925. For the next fifteen years or so, he worked in various manual and unskilled trades, for example as a pedlar, a factory worker, a labourer, and a salesman. He was allowed to remain in Belgium as long as he could provide the appropriate documentation, which, however, had to be renewed at regular intervals – so keeping a clean police record was vital. Uszer's past began to catch up with him in 1925 when a letter arrived from Polish Consulate in Brussels, requesting information from the local police (Sûreté Publique) about the whereabouts of Uszer Frucht, date of birth 20 September 1900, who was wanted for military service in Poland. This generated a small flurry of correspondence over the next two years between Brussels and Charleroi, predominantly concerning whether Ensel and Uszer were indeed one and the same.

It seems that Uszer and the Belgian authorities came to an agreement some time in the mid-1920s that the person hitherto known as Ensel Frucht was to be known officially as Uszer. The name Uszer appeared, for the first time, on Clara's birth certificate in 1927 and then on Augustine's birth certificate in 1930.

A few years passed without incident, and interest in Uszer seemed to wane – until he came to the attention of the authorities once more in 1935, this time for a driving offence. He was charged with driving a car illegally and fined twenty-one francs or a day in prison, with an evident history of minor driving offences behind him. A second enquiry from Brussels in February 1937 served to maintain that interest. The Polish Consulate wished to confirm Uszer's residence in Belgium – in order, it was stated, to 'regularise' his Polish military obligations.

One can only surmise why the Polish authorities were still chasing Uszer, some fifteen years after his supposed desertion. Perhaps a zealous bureaucrat in Warsaw was charged with clearing up outstanding or unresolved cases of desertion from the army or was seeking to recover the fine imposed on those avoiding military service. Unlike the first enquiry, however, this came at the same time as an application from Uszer for renewal of a work permit against the background of recent criminal proceedings against him. Together, they were to set in motion a train of events that ended in Uszer's eventual expulsion from Belgium and that, without a doubt, saved his life.

The 1930s were traumatic years for Belgium as a whole and for the Belgian Jewish community in particular. Of the 110,000 or so Jews living in Belgium on the eve of the Second World War, most had arrived relatively recently – mainly in the five years between 1925 and 1930. This came on the heel of the closure of borders in America, the destination to which most aspired, and before the onset of the Depression, after which would-be migrants into Belgium would have been refused entry. Arriving from Poland, Eastern Europe, and Russia, mainly to escape virulent anti-Semitism and to seek a better life,[64] as in other countries, Jews settled in the larger urban areas such as Brussels, Antwerp, Liege, Charleroi, and Ghent. A minority of Belgian Jews belonged to what might be called the wealthy bourgeoisie. Most were poor, owners of small, family businesses and shopkeepers or, like Uszer, part of the 'mass of [Jewish] hawkers, marketeers and…[small] craftsman'.[65]

During the 1930s, like other workers, Jews lost their jobs. Also as in other countries, they were singled out and scapegoated as most responsible for the economic crisis. One extreme response came from Antwerp, where the middle class, together with the Catholic Church and Catholic Labour Movement, demanded the wholesale expulsion of Belgian Jews.[66] These were dangerous times for Jews, more so for the small minority who were on the left of the political spectrum, like Uszer. The authorities grew increasingly hawk-eyed, as can be seen from their response in 1937 to his application for renewal of a work permit. The application was rejected, so the records show, on the basis that he was a known communist and a subversive. It was noted that he had been president of the Charleroi section of the Soviet-based Prokor and that he had helped organise secret gatherings and had represented Belgium at an international congress. Classed as a revolutionary and militant Jewish activist for nearly a decade, he was, for the first time, given the designation 'undesirable alien'.

As a committed communist and like other comrades, Uszer had indeed been involved in pro-Soviet activities. Among these was the 1932 formation of the Belgian section of Gezerd, an association of Soviet-Jewish nationalist groups and, when it was closed down, its replacement, Prokor. Both organisations occupied a central place in the Jewish community following the closure in 1933 of previously tolerated mainstream Jewish community organisations. Prokor was eventually shut down in 1938, simultaneous with a wave of anti-Semitic arrests and expulsions[67] and at about the same time as arrangements were being made for Uszer's expulsion.

Gezerd, the earlier organisation, has an interesting history. It was established in 1925 in Moscow to plan the establishment of an autonomous Jewish state within the boundaries of the Soviet Union. The idea was an outcome both of Lenin's 'nationality' policy – aimed at providing a territorial home for individual national groups within the Soviet Union where each could pursue cultural autonomy within a socialist framework – and 'territorialism' an early form of Jewish nationalism (similar to Zionism), which wanted a sovereign Jewish state.[68] The creation of such settlements was proposed at various times in locations such as Argentina, Australia, Canada, the United States, and Uganda, as well as Israel.

The Soviet-based experiment, the Birodbidzhan project as it was called, aroused much interest among Jews and non-Jews alike. It was particularly attractive to those who were stateless or vulnerable to persecution or exclusion. For Jewish communists, it was envisioned as a Soviet Zion in which a proletariat Jewish culture could be developed, embedded, and sustained. By the mid-1930s, fifteen thousand settlers had been recruited for Birodbidzhan. Yiddish forms of cultural expression were encouraged, including a Yiddish-language newspaper *Birobidzahner Shtern*, a Yiddish theatre group, and newly built streets named after prominent Yiddish authors. In 1934, the territory was officially elevated to an autonomous region with much optimism for the future. This optimism was short-lived, however. The Soviet Union became increasingly totalitarian under Stalin, and as purges swept the country, attacks were made on the Birodbidzhan leadership, most of who eventually perished. All traces of Jewish culture were gradually erased, so much so that by 1954, a visitor to Birodbidzhan found no indication that there had ever been a Jewish or Yiddish presence.[69] It is easy to see why, both as pro-Soviet and Jewish nationalist in aspiration, Birodbidzhan was attractive to Uszer and his friends, though as with other such utopian projects, it in the end came to nothing.

By May 1937, the Belgian authorities were hot on Uszer's trail. An official's handwritten response to Uszer's lawyer's letter opposing the rejection of a work permit application stated that, in addition to three police cases against him, 'Frucht' had been exposed as a communist sympathiser and 'commissioner' for the Charleroi section of Prokor. In February 1938, Uszer received the shocking news that, after fifteen years of residence in Belgium, he was to be expelled. It should be remembered that the file kept on him was known only to a few officials, and consequently, he would have had little intimation of the developing threat against him.

One can only imagine the despair of Uszer, Ruchla, and the children, along with the wider family, at this decision and the seeming finality of it. Despite pleading letters from Ruchla and Henri, and lawyers' letters protesting against the decision, the expulsion was upheld. Uszer was given notice to leave. Ruchla was also investigated, but though also classed as an immigrant, she had no police record against her and, therefore, was safe from deportation – at least for the moment. Neither was action taken against the children, who were Belgium-born and therefore had automatic right to Belgian citizenship.

On 13 April 1938, Uszer was presented with travel papers valid for fifteen days confirming his expulsion from Belgium, which was to take place at Sterpenish on the Belgian-Luxembourg border. He failed, however, to lodge the papers with the appropriate authorities and, a month later, was reported missing and his description circulated, including the defining characteristic of a half-thumb on his left hand. Pressure was brought on his family to confirm his whereabouts.; the state threatened to withhold payment of Uszer's disability pension. After several months, Uszer was eventually traced to one of the most obvious places that he was likely to choose – the Brussels home of Rivka Demski, sister of his wife Ruchla, and her husband, Charles Zentovsky.

Following this episode, yet more exchanges of letters took place between the Belgian crown prosecutor and Uszer's lawyer concerning the date of deportation and final destination. This period came to a dramatic close early in November 1938, when Uszer was caught by the police, acting on a tipoff, trying to stow away on the S/S *Beaverdale* destined for Canada. He was one of three illegal passengers to be picked up. *Beaverdale* was a Canadian-registered cross-Atlantic vessel, so presumably Uszer's initial target was Canada, although his final intended destination may have been the United States.[70]

Following his arrest, Uszer was charged with 'deceptive boarding' and breaking his deportation order, and imprisoned. The report on this incident signalled a key change to his status. He was now formally identified as a Polish citizen – even though his Polish citizenship had long been revoked (he was, rather, considered by the Poles an army deserter). The following poignant testimony, recorded by the arresting policeman before Uszer was handed over to the Antwerp prison authorities, paints a different picture:

> I met a sailor at the harbour two or three days ago, off the S/S *Beaverdale*. I told him my story. I wanted to find a quiet corner of the earth, and he promised to take me to his ship. On 1 November around midnight, I went with the sailor, whose name I don't

know, to the ship and hid in the bathroom. A police agent found me and took me with two others to the police station. I know that I am to be deported from Belgium as a result of a royal decree dated 23-2-1938. Since that time, I have not left Belgium. I have lived in different places around Belgium. My wife and three children are not to be deported and are still living at 28, rue Brouchetere, Charleroi. I wanted to leave Belgium but I don't have a passport and have lost my Polish citizenship.[71]

Another round of appeals against the expulsion order came to nothing, and after his two-month prison sentence in Antwerp jail came to an end, Uszer's deportation was finally enacted. He was taken on 20 January 1939 to the railway station at Quiévrain, a small town on the Belgian-French border, 20 kilometres west of Mons, and put on a train going west.

We can only speculate what happened next or in the intervening six months before he arrived in London in July. As a fluent French speaker, he was able to merge fairly easily into the background, and as a relatively fit man in his late thirties used to manual labour, he could pick up casual work. We do not know if he remained in France or if he re-crossed the border into Belgium. He told the authorities on his arrival in London that he had been smuggled across the Channel from Antwerp. Perhaps this was the case, or possibly he wanted to ensure that, in the case of deportation, he would be returned to Belgium. Or he might have remained in France and found a passage through Dunkirk or Calais. Whatever his route, he gave himself up to the British authorities on arrival and was instantly indicted for illegal entry. A letter from the British Embassy in Brussels dated 28 September 1939 informed the Belgian authorities of Uszer's arrival and the imminent British deportation order against him. But it also stated that the deportation would not be implemented until confirmation had been received that Uszer would be allowed back into Belgium.

Simultaneously, and demonstrating huge chutzpah and audacity, Uszer sent a letter and later a visa application to the Belgian Embassy, requesting readmission on the grounds of his impending deportation from Britain and his intense wish to be with his family. However, the outbreak of war interrupted both the ensuing correspondence and Uszer's deportation – and that was that, for the time being.

CHAPTER 8

Steffi in London, 1938–1950

At about the same time as Uszer was fighting his deportation from Belgium, Steffi and Elsa were making their way to Dover, arriving in December 1938 on a six-month domestic visa. Trude followed two weeks later on a three-month domestic visa. After months of planning and anxiety, they were finally in Britain and temporarily out of danger, though in a strange country with a strange tongue. There is no information on the route they took from Vienna to London. They might, like many of the Kindertransport[72] children arriving in London a few months later, have taken a train to the Netherlands and then the cross-channel ferry from the Hook of Holland near Rotterdam to a British port, possibly Harwich, and from there to Liverpool Street Station in London. Or perhaps, like many of the refugees interviewed by Maxine Seller in her study of British internees, they made one or more stops en route, in Belgium, Holland, or Luxembourg.[73]

The three Dinger sisters were, of course, enormously relieved to be out of the mayhem that now constituted Jewish life in Vienna though understandably extremely anxious for the people they had left behind, especially their mother. They were also pleased to have arrived at their preferred destination and to be reunited with their London relatives. But London was not what they expected. The country they had just left was in the heart of Europe. It was to other mainland European countries and cultures that Austrians looked for cultural influences and political ideas, rather than across the Channel. Britain to them seemed more engaged with and committed to its empire. Moreover, the London where they found themselves was very different from the Vienna they had left behind. It was winter but not the Austrian winter of snow and clear skies or of clean warm houses. As they explained, the London they first saw was dark and damp, and the houses of their relatives, cramped and badly heated. Why, they asked, were houses constructed so that there was always a draught under the door? Why did the fires give off so little heat yet contrive to spread so much coal dust everywhere?

They were initially euphoric to have escaped and deeply appreciative of the concern and kindness shown to them by their relatives and ordinary British people, as well as by officialdom. But when the euphoria wore off, their anxieties and feelings of dislocation returned. They had expected conditions to be somewhat similar to those in their own country. Indeed, London at the end of the 1939, like Vienna, had suffered from a decade of economic decline, with little money available for the comforts of life, excepting perhaps a weekly visit to the cinema. Heating, as we have seen, was seen to be organised more efficiently in Austria, and British levels of cleanliness were also criticised. The food was strange too, although for those living in Jewish households, there were some reminders of home, derived from the customs and habits of previous migrant generations. Likewise, brought up predominantly on Viennese cuisine, I remember 'English' Jewish food seeming peculiar to me.

Those coming on domestic permits had an altogether harsher life, employed predominantly by non-Jewish (lower) middle-class families who had little understanding or sympathy about the reasons many refugees had exaggerated the extent of their domestic experience and skills.[74] So, there were many instances of dissatisfied employers and confused and miserable employees, though this was not a problem for Steffi and Elsa, who were employed by Fanny – even if only hypothetically. Trude was employed as a domestic servant for some years, however, and by all accounts was unhappy throughout.

As we have seen, in order to guarantee their entry into England, Fanny had invented 'jobs' for the sisters (as laundry maid, mother's help, and so on). She was conscious that she had told less than the truth, perhaps even committed perjury, to help her refugee relatives, and that this might be seen as a very serious offence. I remember Fanny and her family only from the late 1940s onwards, some ten years or more after the Dinger sisters arrived in London and twenty years after Fanny met Steffi in Vienna. I recall Fanny as a buxom, voluble, confident woman, whose presence and personality rather put her husband, Joe, and daughters in the shade – which they seemed not to mind one bit. But I also found Fanny frightening. On the other hand, I greatly looked forward to her renowned Passover meals, to which my mother and I were invited each year. Only much later was I able to identify my occasional discomfort at these times as a feeling of inferiority and unconscious awareness of my mother's and my low status within the wider family hierarchy.

One disadvantage of having Fanny as guarantor was that the Isenstein family itself had very little money, and certainly little was left over from their everyday expenses to support the refugees they had welcomed into their home. As a boy, Fanny's husband, Joe, had gained a scholarship to grammar school. This was so unusual for the time that the whole school had been given a day's holiday in celebration. However, his family had been too poor for him to take up the scholarship, and eventually Joe joined his father's struggling bookbinding business. But business was not his métier as his daughter Mali indicated. 'He was a lousy businessman. He really was. He was much too kind and gentle and nice, and nobody ever paid him. He was always short of money.'[75] On the positive side, Mali added, in those days and in that part of London, there were few people who could be called comfortably off – so there was little sense in the Isenstein household or in my life later on, for that matter, of deprivation or poverty.

The Dinger sisters found themselves welcomed into the Isensteins' small, three-bedroomed, terraced house in North London. Four people – Fanny, Joe, and their two daughters, Mali and Dena – already lived there; another three bodies were difficult to incorporate, with space becoming even more limited when one of Fanny's sisters and her family landed on the doorstop, having been bombed out of their own home. For a time, Steffi shared a bed with Mali, who recalled being much impressed by Steffi's exotic satin nightwear. The space for living was very limited as Mali recalled:

> Our house was very, very small… It was a terraced house. We lived in the kitchen a lot, as one did, because there was no central heating. There was only one fire, so you stayed in the room where it was warm. We had a little garden. As I say, compared with today's standards, it was what you would call an impoverished life.[76]

The Dinger sisters could speak little English, and Mali remembers them talking German to each other, so much so that she managed to pick up many German words in passing. They had brought small gifts for each of the girls – an Austrian national costume (dirndl) comprising embroidered blouse and skirt and apron and several small pieces of jewellery. As a seven-year-old when the Dinger sisters arrived, Mali was much impressed by the gifts but also remembers noticing that the sisters did not look quite right and not at all English. For example, they wore knee-high stockings with short skirts, a strange fashion in London at the time. They also tended to dress more formally than those around them, possibly because their 'best' clothes were all they could take with them when they left Vienna. Anyhow, to Fanny's daughters, their appearance was interesting, strange, and exotic.

So how did the Dinger sisters respond to the hand they had been dealt with? They had escaped from Vienna, it is true, and were safe at last, but they had little money or possessions, no means of support, few possibilities of getting work, only a beginning smattering of English, and a concern not to place Fanny in any danger regarding her guarantor status. They were also deeply anxious about the fate of the people they had left behind, and Mali remembers how much they wept on hearing of the death of their oldest sister, Gisela, in 1940. Until then, Mali said, she had never seen an adult cry. When war came, they were fearful of the bombs and spent many nights sheltering underground at the Manor House tube station nearby, unlike Fanny and her family who preferred the more risky but relative comfort of home. But the Dingers sisters were also fortunate in having each other and Fanny and her family and, therefore, avoided the acute loneliness and feelings of displacement suffered by many other refugees at that time.

Having little to live on, the sisters were advised to seek help with their finances from the German Jewish Aid Committee (GJAC). They were not turned away, much to the credit of the Jewish volunteers responsible for the effectiveness of the system of refugee aid. On seeking help, Steffi was granted two, sometimes three, pounds a month until she found a job and an additional pound a week for nine months in 1940 when she contracted blood poisoning and had to pay for medical treatment. Free medicine on the National Health Service was still some time in the future.

In June 1941, Steffi found work as a leather glove maker, earning two pounds a week. However, a month later, she was again unemployed and seeking work through the German and Austrian Employment Exchange. She was in poor health on and off for the next few years, which was no doubt aggravated by the stress of living in a new country during wartime and, as the news worsened, fear about what was happening in Vienna. Between bouts of illness, she held down various 'blue-collar' jobs such as cap finisher, capstan operator, and machinist, before upgrading as her English improved to office work such as secretary and clerk.[77] Trude had a similar work trajectory. After her unhappy experience as a domestic servant from 1940, she became a cashier in 1944 and then a general office worker. In the early 1960s, she worked as home tutor for 'backward children'. Of the sisters, Elsa was least able to get regular employment due to poor eye sight. She was eventually registered partially sighted, although I recall that, for a time, she worked as a telephone switchboard operator. What enquirers made of her heavy Austrian accent I do not know!

The centre of the sisters' social world in London was not the cramped Isenstein family home but the Finsbury Park branch of the Austrian Centre, which had opened its first premises in Westbourne Terrace in London in March 1939. The Austrian Centre rapidly became the main organisation representing Austrian refugees in Britain and was, for a time, the most important social and support centre for Austrian Jewish refugees in London. But it also had a strong political focus – organising Austrians in the fight against Hitler and building bridges and promoting collaboration with the British.[78] The sisters joined the Finsbury Park branch of the centre soon after it opened, primarily to socialise with other refugees and impose some familiarity on their daily lives. They were also active in the political debates about the future of Austria post-war and, in particular, about what to do when hostilities were over. Should they go back to help rebuild Austria as proposed by the communists? Or should they make their own future in Britain or elsewhere? If the position taken by the sisters is anything to go by, most had a horror of returning. Indeed, my mother and her sisters were never again to set foot in their country of birth. Instead, they opted to remain where they were or to seek to re-migrate to the Unites States of America or some other country that would take them in.

In December 1942, Steffi became, for a few months, the secretary of the Austrian Centre's Finsbury Park branch. An official letter from the Austrian Centre, dated 2 April 1943, to Anthony Eden, then Foreign Secretary and signed by her, is lodged in the National Archives.[79] Though the centre was a broad-based multi-party organisation, whose focal point was predominantly social and cultural, its political voice was shaped largely by Austrian communists, among the earliest refugees to arrive in Britain.[80] Predominantly concerned with internal discussions about the future of Austria, the centre had a reputation for extremism, which was later to cloud Steffi's aspirations for British citizenship.

All three sisters met their future partners or husbands through the centre. First, as we have seen, Steffi met Uszer Frucht, a Polish Jew, previously a coal miner and sometime amateur actor, with whom she set up home and had a daughter. Trude married Johannes Spitz (later anglicised to John Spencer). Trude's husband originally worked in Vienna as an importer/exporter. Then in London he was employed as a railway clerk and, later, as head of an import/export company. The couple had a son, Alexander (Alec), in March 1946. Elsa married Max Mowbray (previously Maximilian Mauruber) in October 1947, following his demobilisation from the British Army. He had escaped to Britain with his first wife before the war, and joined the British Army. Interestingly, following my uploading of material on my family history on my website page, I received a message from Max's first wife's son confirming the details:

> My mother married Maximilian Mauruber in Vienna on 11/07/1936 and divorced him in London on the 23/10/1946. My mother died December last year [2014] aged 99yrs, the only outstanding "fact" I know is she was a relative of Bertha von Suttner [a Czech-Austrian pacifist and novelist, who in 1905 was the first woman to be awarded the Nobel Peace Prize]. We only found out that my mother was a divorcee after our father died. I hope this causes you interest not pain.[81]

This, then was another secret, long kept! After his divorce, Max married Elsa Dinger (see wedding picture below). She had a miscarriage sometime in the late 1940s. He died of a heart attack in 1951 at the age of forty-nine. I remember him as a kind and easy-going uncle who tolerated me playing with his spectacles and stroking his bald patch.

I was seven years old when he died and have only the haziest memory of what happened – but I have never forgotten it. I was woken in what seemed to be the middle of the night to go with my mother to Elsa and Max's apartment on Highbury Hill near the original Arsenal football ground. When we got there, I remember the tears, bleakness, and dark tension in the air. I sensed that something bad had happened but not what it was. Elsa and Max's marriage had not been a happy one, and I was used to witnessing shouting matches and people stomping out of the door. But this time, things were so much worse. It seems that Uncle Max had died suddenly only a few hours earlier, as middle-aged men seemed to do in those days. The detection of heart disease was still in its infancy, as was the NHS. There was a sense of shock and sombreness that even my mother's usually sunny disposition could not hide. One can only imagine the emotions and sadness that Max's death brought, so soon after the loss of so many of the sisters' close and extended family and circle of friends. Certainly for Max's widow, it was a blow from which she never quite recovered.

Towards the end of the war, the sisters became concerned about their status as refugees and their right to remain after hostilities ceased. In 1944, Steffi amended the nationality on her British registration document to Austrian (from German) when Austria was reinstated as an independent country. Elsa and Trude had gained naturalisation (British citizenship) on marriage in Elsa's case and, for Trude, on her husband's naturalisation. Steffi was the only sister to remain stateless – and therefore vulnerable.

Following Uszer's deportation in 1946, Steffi chose to remain in London with her daughter, sisters, and their families, though a report in her Home Office file suggests that, in the early 1950s, she seriously considered emigration to the United States, hoping to live there with Uszer. No doubt, her sister Tilda would have acted as guarantor. However, Steffi would also be aware of the prohibition of known communists from entering the United States. In the end, migration to the States was rejected, and instead, Steffi applied for British naturalisation twice, in 1951 and 1955, unsuccessfully on both occasions. She changed her surname to Frocht by deed pole in 1951, primarily to conceal her daughter's illegitimacy on starting school.

Steffi's failure to gain UK citizenship was due mainly to her continued association with Uszer. The reasons given in her record (though not to her personally) were her relationships with known communists and her own pro-communist beliefs, which she herself denied. We have already learnt about my father's life, the decisions he made, and how they affected the others around him. Here he appears in a minor role. The acting metaphor is deliberate; Uszer was an amateur actor, probably in Poland, certainly in Belgium before the war and in London during wartime. I assume he joined one of the smaller travelling Yiddish theatre groups in London, since I have been unable to find his name on any cast list of the larger companies. Certainly this was the family knowledge that I grew up with.

My mother's first meeting with Uszer was at the Austrian Centre when he was called in to lead a service of remembrance for the dead in the camps. She was secretary of the society at the time so was responsible for the administrative arrangements. Their relationship blossomed, and they moved in together sometime in 1943. Despite all the ups and downs that were to come, she loved him and kept in close contact with him until the time of her death.

When Steffi met him, Uszer was handsome and charismatic as the photograph above indicates. He was, though, less inclined than she, to accommodate to the rigours and hardships of immigrant life. He was frequently out of work and often ill. While they lived together, he relied heavily on Steffi, both financially and domestically. Steffi's youngest sister, Trude, shared with her husband, John, suspicions of Uszer's motives and intentions towards Steffi, feelings that were no doubt heightened when an earlier family was found alive and well in Brussels after the war. Government officials shared this scepticism of Uszer's intentions.

However, despite being active in a Polish Jewish organisation and known as a Communist Party activist during the war, Uszer remained off the government surveillance radar, with interest prompted only by his visa application to visit his Belgian family in 1946. His exit from Britain was swiftly orchestrated. However, it was only when Steffi made her first application for naturalisation in the early 1950s that Uszer's political views came properly to the notice of the security authorities, as did her own.

CHAPTER 9

Uszer in London, 1939–1946

Uszer's time in London is the least known phase of his life, excepting perhaps the first two decades of his life, with only fragmentary evidence available about his London activities and no similar file available to that in Brussels. The Belgian file contains a visa application from Uszer to re-enter Belgium dated late in 1939, which gives a Stepney address, 63 Mansell Street E1, as his London residence. This was the same address as a well-known stopping-off point for Jewish migrants and refugees on the way to their permanent home in the United Kingdom or abroad.[82] Established in the 1890s to provide protection for the first waves of Jewish migrants fleeing the pogroms of Eastern Europe, the Jews' Temporary Shelter (JTS) saw thousands of Jews through its doors and onwards to new and better lives. Headed from 1922 by Otto Schiff, the renowned and influential Jewish banker and philanthropist, the shelter sent representatives to railway stations and ports to meet arrivals and bring them to safety, should they have nowhere else to go. In 1938 and 1939, the organisation helped eight thousand people including, Uszer Frucht.[83] The accommodation offered was temporary – sometimes people stayed for only one night – and Uszer was expected to move on swiftly. However, the archives show that he stayed for some months, which indicates that he had arrived without sponsor or guarantor.

From that point until Uszer's meeting with my mother on 1942 some three years later, I have found no information on his whereabouts or activities. Sometime during this period, he became associated with the Jewish Cultural Club, for Polish émigrés of communist persuasion, and perhaps was provided with accommodation and some payment in exchange for JCC duties. He also joined a 'radical' Yiddish amateur acting group, according to John, Trude's husband.[84] From the early twentieth century onwards, Yiddish was the first language of most Jewish migrants coming to Britain, and Yiddish theatre flourished for some decades in London and the other large cities before gradually dying out in the post-war period. Such groups were dedicated to fostering and preserving Yiddish culture, which was precious to Jewish refugees in transit. And it was in this capacity that Uszer came to the Austrian Centre.[85] Uszer also worked in the tailoring business since he is described as a 'dolly-presser' (ironer of suit sleeves) on my birth certificate.

The only account existing of the initial meeting of Uszer and Steffi is in her letter to her future son-in-law in 1963 (see chapter 13). Uszer, she wrote, was taking part in a service of remembrance when they met at the Austrian Centre to commemorate Jewish victims of the 'gas chambers'. (I am not sure how accurate this is, as not too much was known about the death camps in 1942.) 'My family which were all left behind were threatened with Gas Chambers etc. and Eddi [Uszer] held a Service for the Jewish people under Hitler – so we met.'

When they moved in together, Steffi's two sisters remained in the original jointly shared flat nearby. Perhaps the sisters blamed Uszer for the loss of the company of, and support from, their cherished older sister. Or perhaps they felt he had not earned the trust that Steffi clearly placed in him. For whatever reason, Trude and Elsa were unimpressed by Uszer and retained their suspicions of his intentions towards my mother long after his departure back across the Channel.

The imminent birth of Steffi and Uszer's child was yet another predicament that needed careful handling. Silence, it seems, was the chosen strategy, as letters concerning the birth (which Steffi kept among her papers) express shock and surprise as well as congratulations. For example, a letter from Fanny adopts a somewhat reproachful tone:

> You indeed gave us all a wonderful surprise with the news you wrote. First of all I must congratulate you and your husband [sic] and wish you both MAZELTOV and then hope that you are now feeling better after your long ordeal. I do not know why or what your idea was in 'keeping' the whole matter secret but I suppose your intentions were good.[86]

This apart, there is little to show from Uszer's seven-year sojourn in London, save for various minor glimpses in disparate documentation. For instance, his deportation order to Belgium, though not carried out, is recorded in a Foreign Office file of 1939. His obligation as the family wage earner is questioned in Steffi's German Jewish Aid Committee file (1945–46), and his presence is requested at an interview with a GJAC social worker, Miss Goldschmidt, in 1948 to discuss future plans. There is also an AJR card recording Uszer's 1948 imprisonment in Lewes prison in East Sussex, presumably for entering illegally through Newhaven, which has Steffi as his main British contact. Several letters and postcards exist from him to Steffi, the last sent only some months before she died in September 1969, which indicate the regular communication that she and Uszer maintained. Reports with regard to Uszer's political views and family in Belgium and his undesirability as an illegal alien are summarised in Steffi's Home Office file in response to Steffi's applications for citizenship in the early and mid-1950s. The authorities expressed concern that, should Steffi gain British citizenship and the two were to marry, Uszer could become a permanent problem for years to come.

Surprisingly, Uszer did not come to the attention of the authorities during his stay in Britain in the war years, save in relation to his original illegal entry and after visits he made to Belgium from the mid-1940s to see his first family. Additionally, the branch of MI5 involved in rejecting my mother's applications for naturalisation in the 1950s, as we shall see later, was aware of neither Uszer's political links with the Communist Party and the pro-Soviet Jewish Culture Club while in Britain nor his imprisonment in Lewes in 1948.

It is difficult to gauge from the evidence available, how Uszer handled the personal aspects of his life in London. The clearest accounts have come from the people who knew him and who were still alive to tell the tale at the time I was asking questions. For example, Mali, the oldest daughter of Fanny, a wartime child, recalled Uszer (known to her as Edi) clearly because of his mangled thumb. Mali also remembered her parents accepting Edi and Steffi's relationship. The letter congratulating them on the birth of a daughter, despite the prevailing stigma of illegitimacy and doubts about Edi's dependability and trustworthiness, show this too.

The lengthiest account of Uszer's life in London comes, however, from Steffi's brother-in-law. Trude's husband, John Spencer agreed to be interviewed in 1988, when he was in his eightieth year. I was particularly interested in hearing what he had to say about my father and mother's relationship, since I had gained little from Steffi. John's depiction of Uszer/Edi's entry into Britain largely tallied with that in the Belgian file. For instance, John recalled that Edi had entered illegally from Belgium while the rest of his family remained there and that, as soon as he'd arrived, he had given himself up to the police. The decision was taken to deport him, but this was suspended when war was declared and Belgium was occupied. Edi was eventually given his freedom to live and work in the London area as he wished.

John corroborated Steffi's account of her first meeting with Edi, then an actor in a Yiddish theatre group in London's East End. He said that Edi and Steffi presumed that neither of them would ever again see members of their families left behind. In May 1944, the Austrian Centre received warnings of a catastrophe about to happen in London, most likely the imminent arrival of German flying bombs popularly known as doodlebugs. These first appeared above London on June of that year, in the week of the successful Allied landing in Normandy. At their peak, more than a hundred doodlebugs a day appeared in the skies over south-east England, nearly ten thousand in all. All those who could were pressured to leave London, so Steffi, with baby, and Trude, now married to John, were together evacuated to Leeds. Their partners remained in London, Edi working as a tailor's presser and John as a railway clerk. Edi and John took turns making conjugal visits to Leeds at the weekend. In Leeds, Steffi was involved in a traffic accident – known to me as 'the accident'. She was knocked down by a tram in the blackout and badly injured. After being hospitalised for some weeks, she eventually recovered but was left with a permanent limp and stiff right arm, due she told me, to the poor quality of the Leeds doctors because all the best ones were treating the military.

Eventually, according to John, Edi seemed to settle into his London life, particularly as there was now no fear of deportation. However, when the war ended, he sought to find out what had happened to his family. Much to his surprise and one supposes his joy, it was discovered that, against all odds, they had survived the war. Edi informed Steffi that he needed urgently to travel to Belgium to see if they were alright but, at the same time, promised to set in motion arrangements for a divorce. He made several more visits, which brought him to the attention of the Home Office. It was observed that he was spending more and more time in Belgium. Moreover, some of the trips were no doubt undertaken illegally, as it was comparatively easy in those days to slip unobserved in and out of the country through one or other of the Channel ports.

Trude was even more distrustful of Edi's intentions towards Steffi and their baby daughter – indeed, she suspected him of being a drugs smuggler or worse. Edi was unreliable as a worker, according to John, and frequently ill, and money was tight. Indeed, at various points, Steffi was forced to pawn the little jewellery she had to make ends meet. Significantly, John intimated, Edi's Belgian family was better off economically and more settled socially, which was why he eventually chose to live with them. John could not recall Edi as particularly politically active in London, excepting perhaps as member of his theatre group, which was 'radical' and 'communist inspired'.

Initially, John said, Steffi had approved the trips to Belgium. Eventually, however, it became clear that Edi was dividing his time between the two families. As can be imagined, this caused huge tensions within the London-based family; this was less so in Belgium, as Edi had revealed little to his Belgian family about his London experiences. He was more concerned with defending himself from accusations that he had deserted his Belgian family to enjoy a relatively easy time in London during the war.

In the end, on realising that he had somewhere to go, the Home Office intervened, and Edi was given three months to leave. He departed from London in 1946, leaving behind his common-law wife and two-year old daughter. Steffi changed her name by deed poll to Frocht believing this was no more than a technicality until his divorce came through and that he would do the right thing and leave his wife.

CHAPTER 10

Amalia and Frieda: Lodz, Terezin, and Treblinka

In 1938, 206,000 Jews were living in Vienna, 10 per cent of the Viennese population. Of those, over half (130,000) left the country before the war started, the three Dinger sisters included, and nearly a third (65,000) died or were murdered in ghettos and camps of one sort or another. Among those who died were Steffi's mother, Amalia, and aunt, Frieda. There were fewer than 2,000 survivors and even fewer who remained or returned to Vienna after the war.[87]

How did these things happen? How did the route to destruction and mass murder take place? Until 1941, the Nazis, who had been in power in Austria since 1938, were mostly interested in encouraging Jews to emigrate, providing, as we have seen in the case of Steffi and her sisters, they left behind most of their possessions. Also as noted, many countries refused to accept Jewish refugees. Those that did operated a tight quota system. What were the Nazis to do with those Jews who remained, mainly because no one would take them in?

Initially, various plans aimed at 'resettling' the Jews were discussed – one proposed destination was the island of Madagascar in the Indian Ocean – but all were discarded by Nazi leaders. It was decreed that, at all costs, Germany and its conquered territories should become Jew-free. Jews – alongside other 'unwanted' groups, such as Roma, gypsies, and political opponents – were first deported to 'transit' camps and ghettos in the East as slave labour for the Nazi war machine. There, they died of ill treatment, starvation, or worse. Later, the focus switched to mass murder so that, by mid-1941, after the German invasion of the Soviet Union, the SS and police mobile units were testing out new forms of ensuring collective death. Using panelled mobile trucks with exhaust pipes reconfigured to pump poisonous carbon monoxide into sealed spaces, they entered into killing sprees aimed at eliminating entire communities in the occupied countries. These were designed to complement previous and ongoing shooting operations.

Four weeks after the beginning of the invasion of the Soviet Union and as the Germans advance westwards gained pace, Hitler allocated responsibility for state security to SS chief Heinrich Himmler, which included plans for the elimination of perceived threats to permanent German rule. Following this, Hermann Goering (Hitler's deputy) authorised General Reinhard Heydrich to make preparations for the implementation of a 'complete solution of the Jewish question', code-named Aktion Reinhard.

On 20 January 1942, thirteen senior Nazi and German officials took part in a meeting on the shore of Lake Wannsee, a few miles from Berlin. Convened by Heydrich, the meeting had one primary purpose – to secure support from, and coordinate involvement of, German government ministries and other agencies in the mass murder of Jews. Legitimation, if one can use such a word in such a context, came with news that Hitler himself had approved the operation. Thus the aim of the Wannsee Conference was not to debate whether such an action should be undertaken but to discuss how, where, and when. Present at the meeting were the officials responsible for the disposal of Jewish property, plus Adolph Eichmann, in charge of the Gestapo's Jewish affairs section and Heinrich Müller, Gestapo chief. Agreement was reached so quickly that the entire business was completed in under a day.[88]

The Nazis were clearly aware of the public lack of appetite for mass murder since Aktion Reinhard was carried out in the utmost secrecy, with every effort made not to alert the populace to its overall aim.

The first stage was notice of deportation. Some potential deportees chose to ignore or evade transportation. Among these was the extraordinary Marie Jalowicz, one of only 1,700 Jews who managed to survive in Berlin through the war years. Marie was helped by many different people, Jews and non-Jews alike, and her account suggests that there were many who opposed the Nazis regime. A young woman with enormous energy and determination, she went underground and, on one occasion, outwitted the Gestapo when they came for her by escaping dressed only in her petticoat in the middle of winter.[89] Tilda, Steffi's younger sister, likewise refused to accept deportation and decided instead to make a sometimes harrowing journey eastwards from Vienna, finally reaching the United States just before war broke out in the Pacific. However, for older people, those with large families, or with few cultural or financial resources, evading capture was more difficult. Marie Jalowicz's Aunt Grete was among the first in Berlin to receive a deportation order, late in 1941. Having spent the final few days before the deportation with her aunt, during which she reminisced as she destroyed various photographs, the young Marie felt relief as well as sadness when it was all over. 'I felt unspeakably sorry for her, and I would have so much liked to help, but I couldn't bear it any more. I was even a little relieved when it was all over.'[90] Eventually, deportation was to become normalised as an everyday, even if unwelcome, occurrence.

So it was likely for older deportees to be more resigned, exhausted no doubt by the whole process of Nazification. When served with a deportation order, a person was typically informed that he or she was being sent away to work. Advised to bring clothing, blankets, shoes, eating utensils (but no knife), bowl, and some money, these people were rounded up and put into trucks or marched to a nearby railway station. Trains carrying deportees were deliberately parked at a distance from the usual passenger terminals, out of the eye of the local populace. Initially, and this was the case in Vienna, deportees travelled in ordinary passenger trains. Later, cattle trucks were used, as conditions became more brutal and inhumane.

We, of succeeding post-war generations, are familiar with and perhaps have become impervious to, such stories of deportation, horror, and murder. However, when applied to people that we have come to know, the stories take on a more personal and intimate nature, and it is easier to understand the impact of such terrors on humanity. We begin to appreciate what it must have felt like to people like ourselves, people like Amalia and Frieda. The bare facts we know concerning these two women's fates, taken from the Yad Vashem Holocaust Museum's website, are as follows:

Frieda Beila Dinger (maiden name: Moskovicz)
- Born 08-07-1877
- Wartime address: Wien 2, Krummbaumgasse 2/12
- Details of transport: From Vienna to Litzmannstadt (Lodz) and to Lodz Ghetto on 02-11-1941, address, Rembrandtstrasse, 4 Flat 19
- Prison number on Transport: 277

Victim's status: Perished

Malke Dinger
- Born 04-11-1873 in Brody
- Wartime address: Wien 2, Krummbaumgasse 2/12
- 1st transport: No. 34 from Vienna to Theresienstadt Ghetto, Czechoslovakia, 29-07-1942, prison no. 6-942
- 2nd deportation: To Treblinka Camp, Poland, 26-09-1942

Victim's status: Perished

Frieda

Frieda went first, on 2 November 1941, one of 998 deportees to Lodz, just like Marie's Aunt Grete a month or so before.[91] We do not know exactly what happened to Frieda, but existing testimony from survivors gives us a good idea.[92] She would be selected on the basis of a priority list. If the selection was alphabetical, Dinger would have been one of the first selected. Perhaps this was not the case here, though, as her older sister, Amalia, was not destined for the same transport. Frieda would have been asked to report to a local holding centre, often the local school, where mattresses and food would be provided by the Jewish community. She might have had to wait some hours, although for a few it could take days and weeks, before she was allocated by the officer in charge to her place of destination, Lodz. Others were sent to Riga or Terezin. She would have been bundled on to a huge truck destined for Aspenbahnhof, the station serving trains to the east. Testimony suggests that she would have travelled on an ordinary train at this time, since cattle trucks had not yet become the main mode of transport for deportees. She would also have received food for the journey prepared beforehand by local Jewish community groups.

Lodz (known also by its German name Litzmannstad) lies north of the Austrian border in what is now the Czech Republic. The journey would not have taken long – perhaps a few hours. Security was tight, but the journey might have been, to some extent, reassuring. Frieda was allowed to take only her basic possessions, although she may have sewn small pieces of jewellery in her coat lining or hidden money in her clothing, as others did. After all, she did not know when and if she would return. At this time, she would have had little idea of what was to come. She may have hoped that she would avoid in the work camp the routine discrimination and humiliation that faced her daily in Vienna. She may even have volunteered to go, which would explain her early departure.

What was this Lodz Ghetto, Frieda's final residence? Few survived, so we cannot know her precise experience. We can be sure that, as soon as she arrived at the station, she would have become aware she had been naive to raise her expectations. Rather than the formally polite officers she was used to dealing with in Vienna, noise, guards, and barking dogs would have confronted her upon her arrival at Radogoszcz (Radegast) station, the main entry point for the Lodz Ghetto. The process had been carried out before, with the various transports of Jews and Gypsies in 1941 from outside Poland and, later, the waves of Jewish communities brought in from liquidated ghettoes of towns and villages in the surrounding region. She would have been processed, her name checked and her belongings searched, and any discovered jewellery or other precious possessions would have been confiscated. She was then led to a holding bay (old school building or the like) before being allocated to an already crowded ghetto apartment. We can see from the record above that she lived (and probably died) on Rembrandtstrasse, at number 4, flat 9. From October 1941 onwards, it was the allocated housing area for Jews from Austria and Czechoslovakia, predominantly from Vienna and Prague. It was also the location of a central soup kitchen as well as the ghetto's tailoring sector and central depot for raw materials. So Frieda may have been put to work as a tailor at No. 8 Rembrandtstrasse, not far from where she lived.

The Lodz Ghetto was established as an economic unit for the Nazi war machine, as well as to enable the persecution and elimination of Jews and other undesirables. Inmates had neither legal protection nor proper food and accommodation, so living conditions were poor from the beginning. The ghetto in Lodz was established in April 1940, following the Nazi invasion of Poland. The most neglected part of town with the poorest living conditions was selected for the site, already the home of around 62,000 Jews. Non-Jews were forcibly evicted, and the 100,000 or so Jews living in other parts of the city and its suburbs were forced in. This was followed by a wholesale seizure of Jewish-owned properties, furnished apartments, and works of art. Some two weeks after this forced movement of people, the ghetto was enclosed with barbed wire and a police guard installed. Inmates were forbidden to leave and anyone who entered or left the ghetto without permission or was caught smuggling was summarily shot. The same fate awaited anyone who approached the perimeter fence without permission.

The organisation of the Lodz Ghetto with its German-led administration (Ghettoverwaltung); various policing organisations (the Gestapo, Kripo, and Schupo[93]); and so-called Jewish self-government (elders, here led by Mordechai Chaim Rumkowski) became a prototype for other ghettos and camps. The role of Rumkowski and others like him was to ensure that the Jewish inmates obeyed the rigid and brutal regime of the ghetto. Elders also took decisions about work allocation, food distribution, and ghetto 'welfare'. Rumkowski, for example, was responsible for the internal organisational structure of the ghetto and its policing by Jewish security guards. He also liaised directly with the Nazi chief of police. Those working for Rumkowski were rewarded with a larger food ration and temporary protection from deportation – so competition to join his administration was fierce. The main area of work was the production of German Army uniforms. If an individual could not work, she or he would receive no food, with certain death to follow. The role played by Rumkowski was made even more difficult by the fact that he was required to make decisions about selections for deportation to death camps such as Chelmo. A horrific example occurred in September 1942 when the Nazis demanded twenty thousand deportees to be taken from the elderly and very young, the least economically productive. Rumkowski made what has become an infamous speech on the day of the selection, pleading for understanding:

> A grievous blow has struck the ghetto. They are asking
> us to give up the best we possess – the children and
> the elderly... I must stretch out my hand and beg:
> Brothers and sisters, hand them over to me! Fathers
> and mothers, give me your children.[94]

Rumkowski said that, if such decisions were not taken by him and other ghetto inmates, the Germans themselves would carry out the selection, more forcibly and more brutally. He declared that he had always worked for peace, 'but something else, it turns out, was destined for us'. Many have judged him a collaborator, responsible for a demoralised and ultimately deadly camp organisation, and blamed him for easing the process of Nazi selection and deportation to the death camps. Others have viewed him as a pragmatist who did the best he could to save lives and alleviate suffering and as a martyr, who ultimately suffered the same fate as everyone else. Following the liquidation of the ghetto in 1944, Rumkowski and what was left of his family were transported to, and then murdered in, Auschwitz.

About a third of the Lodz Ghetto population died from the harshness of the conditions (from starvation, lack of hygiene, cold, and so on). The remainder were murdered, mainly gassed, during four main deportation periods – December 1941, when 20,000 Jews were sent to the Chelmno death camp; January to September 1942, when 70,000 were gassed, including the designated elderly and children; June to July 1944, when 7,000 Jews perished; and from August 1944 onwards, following the liquidation of the ghetto, when 60,000 Jews were transported and murdered, this time in Auschwitz. A clear-up squad of about 750 Jews was left behind. They, along with 30 children and 80 adults in hiding, were eventually liberated by the Soviet Army on 19 January 1945. The killing machine was in operation right up to the end.

Eventually some retribution was exacted. Hans Biebow, the ghetto director for its entire duration, was tried, found guilty of crimes against humanity, and summarily executed in Lodz in April 1947.

As for Frieda, she was among nearly 5,000 inmates sent from Vienna, only 34 of whom survived to the liberation of the Lodz Ghetto and other nearby camps.[95] These tended to be young people, whose bodies and minds were capable of withstanding the crippling conditions that confronted them. Frieda was 67 when she arrived, and however fit she may have been, her age limited the kind of work she could do and her ability to survive. She may have worked for a short time in tailoring, but if or when she fell behind, starvation was the inevitable outcome since, as far as we know, she had no relatives or friends to sustain or protect her. Since she is not listed in the deportations, she died within the ghetto – of starvation, disease, German brutality, despair, and/or all of these.

Amalia

On receiving her notice of deportation to Terezin, Amalia's experience was similar to that of her younger sister. This took place on 29 July 1942, about eight months after Frieda. Likewise, she was asked to present herself at the local meeting point for collection. She was allowed to take with her only a few possessions and required to turn in the key of her flat, so that others could move in. We can see from the record that another woman from the same building, Tini Steiner, born 1862 and therefore aged eighty at the time, left on the same transport. Perhaps Amalia helped her older neighbour to prepare herself for the journey. Or she may have travelled with others from the house, since, altogether, twenty-eight Jews from the apartment house in which she lived were deported and perished.

Like Frieda before her, Amalia was unlikely to have known the precise situation into which she was being forced, although by now, some months after the transports began, she was no doubt resigned to the probability of further horrors to come. The distance between Vienna and Terezin is around four hundred kilometres. According to survivors, the journey took about twenty-four hours by rail. Again, conditions on the train were tolerable by all accounts, even for the elderly. The true horror of her situation would not have been revealed until the train reached its destination, Bauschovitz, several kilometres outside the ghetto. Deportees were typically force-marched to the ghetto, although the elderly and infirm were often taken in trucks. This might have been the case for Tini, if not for Amalia.

The first impression Amalia would have gained of Terezin was of a high brick wall topped with grass and surrounded by a moat. She would have been marched alongside other deportees through a wall gate into an area, where they were searched for hidden and 'illegal' possessions and then sent to a former barracks to wait until allocated a place to stay. Amalia was in Terezin for a little less than two months. She had time to get to know the organisation of the camp and gain a sense of where her future might lie.

Originally a garrison town founded in 1780 by Emperor Joseph II in honour of his mother, the Empress Maria Theresa, Terezin was transformed into a ghetto with the arrival of the first Jewish deportees on 24 November 1941. It was used to house mainly elderly Jews who could not be sent as forced labour to the main work camps in the east. Included among the inmates were 'invalids, those over sixty-five, decorated and disabled war veterans, those in mixed marriages and their children, and prominent Jews...who had connections'. [96] Alongside instructions about Aktion Reinhardt, Heydrich had announced at the Wannsee conference that Terezin was to be a special Jewish ghetto, a showcase to the world of German's benign treatment of the Jews. Indeed, the Red Cross was notoriously misled by a carefully orchestrated visit in June 1944.

Previously, Jews had been sent to Poland or Russia, as in the case of Frieda. But later, in 1942, Terezin was reimagined as a more 'privileged' ghetto for the 'deserving'. It never lost its original purpose however – as a transit camp for Jews en route to the east. Even if its mortality rate was slightly lower than the worst of the other camps and ghettos, statistics are revealing. Of the 140,000 who entered the walled town between November 1941 and March 1945 when it was liberated, almost 90,000 were sent to their deaths in Auschwitz, Treblinka, and other killing factories. Of the remaining, 33,000, mainly children and the elderly, died from the hardships of living in the ghetto. Only 16,832 survived; many of them had entered the camp late in the war, when conditions had begun to improve (in preparation for the Red Cross visit in 1944) and when deportations had all but ceased.

The first and most sadistic commandant of the ghetto, Siegfried Seidl, directed frequent beatings of inmates and ordered the only formal executions there, in 1942. Seidl was replaced in June 1943 on the orders of Adolf Eichmann. His evident sadism was felt to be out of tune with the new image of Terezin. Seidl's successor, Anton Burger, remained in charge of the ghetto until a month before the Russians arrived. The organisation of Terezin was similar to that of Lodz, with Jewish elders acting as leaders of the Jewish ghetto community. Under Burger's rule, there were three Jewish leaders – Jakob Edelstein, who was deported east with 5,000 of his fellow Czechs in December 1943; Paul Eppstein, who was murdered by the Nazis in September 1944 on the eve of the last wave of deportations to Auschwitz; and, for the last few months, Benjamin Murmelstein, with the renowned Leo Baeck as his deputy. Both survived the war.

Under Burger's supposedly more benign rule, several hundred people died in a single night (11 November 1943) when the camp's entire population of forty thousand was forced to stand outside all night in the freezing cold for a 'census count'. As in Lodz, the number of people transported eastwards was dictated by the Nazis, but the burden of selection was placed on the Jewish elders. As Norbert Troller, a Terezin survivor, laments:

> In the end this unbearable, desperate, cynical burden destroyed the community leaders who were forced to make the selections. The power over life and death forced on the Council of Elders was the main reason, the unavoidable force, behind the ever-increasing corruption in the ghetto; its single, solitary goal was life and 'protection' from transports.[97]

As the population of the Terezin Ghetto increased, transports east began. The first, on 11 March 1942, was to Lublin, a forced work camp in Poland, and then onwards to instant death at Bełżec and Sobibór concentration camps. [98] The first transport to Treblinka, about fifty miles North East of Warsaw, took place on 19 September 1942. Tini was on the second on 21 September, and Amalia was on the fourth, on 26 September. These initial transports out of Terezin were mainly for carrying the elderly, although younger Jews occasionally were assigned to them.

Hershl Sperling, for example, was only fifteen when he was packed onto the same train as Amalia to Treblinka. The Gestapo had discovered Hershl and his family hiding in a bunker in Czestochowa nearby, only several hours before. Hershl wrote of the terrible thirst of people in the freight car, the desperate souls crammed in like cattle, and the sweet odour of death that hovered over Treblinka as the train pulled in towards its destination.[99] There were 2,004 people crammed into the carriages, with the bodies of those who died en route left in the carriages, so that the number on arrival would match that of departure. Much has been written about Treblinka that I do not want to include here – details about how and where the trains were stopped; the extreme secrecy of the operations; the heart-breaking cries for help and water from the entrapped Jews to the local peasants; the enforced shearing of hair and stripping of clothes before deportees were harried, whipped, and rushed into the gas chambers, all achieved within a couple of hours. The only people to survive Treblinka were the Nazi instigators, their Ukrainian collaborators, and usually for only a few hours, the young men selected from the deportees to dispose of bodies.

The commandant of Treblinka for most of its existence, was Franz Stangl, formerly an Austrian policeman and non-Nazi. He was appointed commandant of the Sobibór death camp and then of Treblinka, due to ambition, involvement in the earlier German euthanasia programme, and coercion. He escaped at the end of the war, eventually arriving in Brazil, but was tracked down by Nazi hunter Simon Wiesenthal and arrested by the Brazilian police in February 1967. He was condemned to life imprisonment in 1970 but died only six months into his sentence.

Interviewed by the journalist Gitta Sereny in 1971 some weeks before his premature death, Stangl expressed considerable remorse about what had happened. He explained that the only way he could tolerate what he had been asked to do was to disassociate himself mentally from the camp's principal activity. His main tasks, he saw, were administration and paperwork and to ensure efficiency and the minimisation of camp corruption. He described 'work' in the following way:

> Of course, as I said, usually I'd be working in my office: there was a great deal of paperwork – till about

eleven. Then I made my next round [the first was at 5.00 a.m.] starting on top of the *Totenlager* [disposal of dead bodies]. By that time they were well ahead with the work up there.

Sereny explained:

What he meant was that by this time the 5,000 people who had arrived that morning were dead: the 'work' he referred to was the disposal of the bodies, which took most of the rest of the day. I knew this but I wanted to get him to speak more directly about the *people* and asked where the people were who had come on the transport. But his answer was evasive: he still avoided referring to them as people.

Sereny pursued Stangl's ability to dehumanise the victims of the process for which he was responsible, by avoiding meeting them, and by viewing them primarily as 'cargo'. He responded:

I think it started the day I first saw the *Totenlager* in Treblinka. I remember Wirth [a leading Aktion Reinhardt protagonist] standing there, next to these pits full of blue black corpses. It had nothing to do with humanity – it couldn't have: it was a mass – a mass of rotting flesh. Wirth said 'What shall we do with this garbage?' I think unconsciously that started me thinking of them as cargo.[100]

For Amalia, only a very small part of Stangl's 'cargo', Treblinka marked the end of her life and her suffering. She may have died on the journey to the camp due to her weakened state after Terezin. Or she may have survived to meet her fate in the gas chambers. She was sixty-nine.

Who was left to mourn her passing? It was not until her daughters in London in 1947 made a request to the UK Search Bureau based in Bloomsbury that they or anyone else were notified of Amalia's death. Below is the short, shocking note that they received, nearly five years after the event.

Given the news that had come out of the camps, Steffi, Elsa, Trude, and eventually Tilda in America presumably were not surprised to hear confirmation of the death of their mother. Thankfully for them, the absolute horror of the camps and ghettos would not be revealed for some years into the future. Amalia was also mourned by the world as one of six million Jews who perished for one reason only – their Jewish heritage – in what came to be known as the Holocaust.

CHAPTER 11

Uszer in Brussels, 1946–1980

For Uszer, the most significant factor of the immediate post-war period was his persistence in finding a way of getting back to Belgium – despite his promises to and espoused affection for Steffi. From documentation in his Belgian file, we can see that, as soon as armistice in Europe was declared, he made an urgent visa request to the Belgian Embassy due, so he said, to his deeply held wish to be back with his family. He was initially granted a three-week visa (deadline, 15 January 1946) and forbidden to stay longer, despite a character reference from the Jewish Victims of War organisation in Brussels. Following a round of correspondence between the family, a lawyer, and the Belgian authorities, predominantly concerning the poor health of his wife, Uszer was granted a second visa, this time for three months (deadline, 3 July 1946).

Once in Brussels, he began to campaign for permanent residence. It is clear that what he wanted most was to be with his 'first' family, despite assurances to Steffi of his intention to initiate divorce proceedings. In the end, the decision was taken out of his hands. He overstayed his three months' visa time limit. This brought him to the notice of the British authorities, who concluded that he had found somewhere else to stay outside Britain. Following his deportation, he was granted temporary residence in Belgium. Two years later, in 1948, he gained the right to remain permanently, this time as a stateless person rather than Polish citizen.

Together with Ruchla, Uszer was issued a permit in October 1948 to open a shop in Brussels, selling newspapers, confectionary, and fabrics. Gradually his reputation was restored. There were no further reported incidents or political indiscretions, save for a couple of minor infringements, for example, a five-franc fine in 1949 for bad behaviour, a query about the shop's labelling practices, and several minor driving offences. There was always some tension (evidenced in his file) around the time that working permit applications were due for renewal, with some internal debate among Belgium officials about whether he should be allowed to stay. After some years, the shop failed, and Uszer got a job with the same brother-in-law who had hidden him from deportation in 1938 and who now owned a successful clothing factory making denim jeans. The renewal process for work permits was no longer crucial.

Uszer took on the designation of 'businessman' – although not an altogether successful one according to his Belgian offspring. Such a role, however, provided him with a useful cover, for example, when making surreptitious visits to Britain in the 1950s and 1960s.

The only other noteworthy event at this time was a request in 1967 from the Association of Political Prisoners in Silesia[101] for Uszer to attend a memorial ceremony at Auschwitz as a United Nations' refugee. This was granted, confirmed by a postcard from him in my possession from the former death camp with the scrawl, 'I'm in Poland. I went to see the museum of the dead from our People. Never forget. Never forget'.

In March 1972, Uszer began the process of applying for Belgian citizenship, which was finally granted in July 1974. Following this, his wife applied for and was granted similar citizenship rights. Uszer Frucht died on10 May 1981 in his eighty-first year. His wife, Ruchla Demski, died seven years later in 1988.

And so...

What can be made of this life? To what extent is it possible to come to know this person, this character whose life traversed the short and terrible twentieth century? Like most of our own lives, Osher/Uszer/Ensel/Eddi/Edi's life was necessarily shaped by the times and spaces though which he lived. He was political firebrand and ideological force in his younger years in Poland; migrant, worker, and political organiser in his late twenties and thirties in Belgium; and fugitive, living on his wits, in his last years in Belgium. He was temporary resident and new parent in London; unremarkable businessman upon his return to Belgium; and, towards the end of his life, tenacious Belgian citizen.

If nothing else, it must be acknowledged that he was a resolute survivor. Despite all his travails before, during, and after the war and despite the fact that he smoked and drank with gusto throughout his life, he lived into his eighties, outlasting his wartime 'wife' Steffi by more than a decade. He never deviated from his commitment to communism, despite various political crises within communism, including the fall of Stalinism, the Hungarian Uprising, and the criticisms and lack of sympathy from his wife's relatives and his children in Belgium. He was able to enjoy a good quality of life in post-war Belgium, sustained by the business acumen of his wife's family. He also managed to maintain the affections and loyalty of the two women who bore him children and was evidently a charming, if unreliable and sometimes deceitful, spouse and partner.

In writing Uszer's part of the story, I had two questions. As his daughter, I wanted to understand what his life meant to me personally. And as the narrator of his life, I was interested in, first, the possibility of his life as indicative of the lives of many others who were implicated in the two world wars and ideological clashes of the twentieth century, and, second, the extent to which he was able to exercise agency and take ethical decisions that affected others. If he was indeed a deserter from the Polish military, were his reasons for leaving political, economic, personal, or a mixture of all of them? On being given notice of his deportation from Belgium in 1938, did he have a plan? Or did he just head for the hills? On discovering that his wife and children had survived the war, did he take a decision to return permanently to Belgium? Or did he try to keep his options open as long as possible –trying not to hurt too many people? Did he feel an element of responsibility for his London family? Or did he consciously and cynically choose to leave for the better economic and social conditions that his Belgian family could offer?

If this is 'authorized fiction' as Nadel suggests, as author I should perhaps determine the answers to these questions. The feeling I have gained from the documents, papers, and testimony about him is that Uszer was an intelligent and passionate man who found himself on the right (or rather left) side of politics and on the wrong side of the law in Poland and who sought a way out by finding work on the other side of Europe. When his work as a miner was curtailed accidentally, in circumstances beyond his control, he sought for the next ten or so years in Belgium both to provide for his growing family and to maintain his commitment to a form of revolutionary politics. He did not know of his emerging profile as dangerous revolutionary and Jewish activist, as indicated in his Belgian police file. Nor was he aware of the case being mounted by the Belgian authorities for his expulsion. When the accusations surfaced, he did his best to repudiate them. Nevertheless, he was one of many who were expelled by the reactionary and increasingly anti-Semitic governments of the time, due to political convictions, religion, or migrant status. Having no-one left to turn to in Belgium and with nowhere to go and one failed attempt to get away behind him, he eventually found his way to London. His last desperate attempt to return legally to his family in Belgium was thwarted by the start of war hostilities.

Stranded in London for the duration of the war, he decided to make the best of it. He joined one or more of the Polish left-wing migrant and/or Jewish organisations that proliferated at the time, the consequence of the presence of the many refugees who were similarly stuck in limbo in London. He joined a Yiddish acting troupe and met my mother. They fell in love at a febrile time when, as she put it, the world was 'topsy-turvy'.

However, I also have the impression that he was never 'comfortable' living the British way of life – 'inside rather than outside the home' as he once said to me. He found wartime London cold, wet, and unfriendly, though I do believe that he had genuinely loving feelings for my mother. On unexpectedly finding his first family alive, and like anyone else with emotions and perhaps feelings of guilt, he wanted urgently to check the state they were in and see what he might do to help them. My impression is that, once back in Belgium, he developed a sense of comfort and belonging that had been missing in London. More so, his wife's family were more affluent, and he may have anticipated that life in Brussels would be less of a struggle there than it would in London.

Whatever he might eventually have decided, the British authorities intervened and threw him out. He was stuck once more, this time in Belgium. At this time, he had two alternatives. He could come clean to his wife and family about what had happened in London and risk the possibility of being evicted from the family home and possibly the country. Or he could keep his London family secret but do as much as possible to help them. He chose the latter, and this was where his acting skills came in. He was able to orchestrate ways in which he could get time away, for instance as reported by his children, by initiating huge arguments at home and disappearing to stay with 'friends' for a few days or claiming to have business commitments that required him to be elsewhere.

I imagine that he was fond of both his Brussels and London families, but circumstances dictated that he could not have both. Whatever the reason, he stayed in Belgium for the rest of his life. Nevertheless, he had the ability to make my mother feel loved until the day she died, arranged regular meetings with us, and was even properly attired as the father of the bride at my wedding in 1963. He was certainly shocked and saddened when my mother died. No doubt, he would have continued to maintain contact with me following her death had I wanted to. Whether this might have led to earlier acknowledgement by the Belgian family of Uszer's London family or a better fusing together of his two separate lives is something that we shall never know.

To what extent Uszer's life emulates that of others caught up in the major twentieth-century European conflicts is difficult to ascertain. He survived when many did not – in times and places that were antithetical to his existence as a Jew and as a communist. He was to some extent lucky. For example, had he not been expelled from Belgium, he would no doubt have been among the first to be rounded up when the Nazis invaded. He was deeply challenged by the forces ranged against him but had sufficient chutzpah and quick-wittedness to find spaces in which to survive. He never gave up – either on his politics or his various entanglements and relationships. Perhaps this is one of several characteristics that he passed on to me and on which I have drawn in pursuing his story.

CHAPTER 12

Steffi and Whitehall, 1950–69

Like most other refugees from Nazi Europe who could not or did not want to return after the war, and following Uszer's departure, Steffi sought to secure her right to stay permanently in Britain. The most common way of achieving this was to apply for British citizenship, then known as naturalisation. Had either of her two applications for naturalisation in 1951 and 1954 been successful, the documentation would not have been available for me to trace what happened and what arguments were given for and against her naturalisation. Further, the role of the secret services in Steffi's later life would not have become apparent. From Steffi's Home Office file, we can see that her applications brought her to the attention of MI5, with negative consequences in the end for her desired status as a British citizen.

Why MI5 came to be involved in Steffi's case was something of a mystery to me. Who were these so-called security authorities? And why were their actions so influential in the early 1950s? From consulting Christopher Andrew's blockbuster on the history of MI5, *The Defence of the Realm*, I learnt that foreign intelligence had only become an issue for the British government at the beginning of the twentieth century and was then a marginal and somewhat amateur enterprise. First based in premises directly opposite the Army and Navy Stores in central London and rented in the name of a private detective, retired Chief Inspector Edward 'Tricky' Drew, the Secret Service Bureau (SSB) was originally set up to deal with the threat posed by German espionage before and during the First World War.[102] Following the Armistice and perceived reduction of the German threat, the service was gradually run down, such that, at the end of the 1920s, its very existence was under threat. However, following the dramatic discovery of the penetration of Police Special Branch by Soviet intelligence in 1929, it began to expand once more. Curiously, no prosecutions came as a result of the 1929 security breach. Two officers were dismissed and responsibility for counter-espionage was shifted to MI5, the part of the service concerned with internal national security.[103]

From then on, the Soviet Union and international communism became the main target of MI5's attentions. It was only slowly, late in the 1930s, that the dangers from British fascism and the Nazi regime were recognised. The service expanded in numbers and scope to meet the challenge, to a wartime peak in 1943 of 332.[104] Deep frustration was expressed by agents, however, at having to devote so much time to surveillance of enemy aliens inside Britain, instead of addressing the external threats posed by German intelligence and the necessity for counter-espionage.

MI5 surveillance of communists inside Britain, including those from Germany and Austria, continued seamlessly into the post-war period, when concern abounded about the extent of the Red Threat and the influence of the Soviet Union. Extensive surveillance was carried out, in particular on British Communist Party contacts with foreign communists.[105] In the 1950s, with the Soviet bloc ensconced in Eastern Europe and McCarthyism at its height in the United States of America, it was perhaps not surprising that relationships between communists or fellow travellers, such as my mother and father, would become a target of scrutiny. Also, the Austrian Centre was a major Secret Service irritant, perceived as predominantly communist-inspired and led and continually targeted for closure.

Steffi's unsuccessful attempts to gain citizenship are illuminating in several ways. For a short time, it seemed that most of her file would remain unread; the only documentation initially released to me covered Steffi's arrival in Britain, excluding the extensive documentation associated with her naturalisation applications. The latter documents were designated 'closed' until 2069. On appeal, I was given access to the entire file, apart from a few redacted names (of informers). I found the following short narrative about Steffi, which had been constructed jointly by Police Special Branch and MI5:

> She [Steffi] had been an Austrian refugee who had been granted a six-month visa to enter the country, arriving on 8 December 1938. She had co-habited with Mr Usyer [**][106] Frocht (born 20.9.1900.) from 1943–6, with whom she had an illegitimate daughter. They had intended to marry, once he had divorced his wife. Mr Frocht was a Russian [**] who, on being expelled from Belgium in 1939, then had entered the UK illegally. His deportation order was not enforced and eventually it was revoked in 1946. In the same year, he visited his wife and three children in Belgium and subsequently was refused re-entry into the UK. He later moved alone to France [**] where he resided from about 1950 onwards. He continued to receive short annual [**] visits from Steffi, who travelled abroad to see him. By 1950, Steffi was living alone with her daughter.

There were clear errors. For example, Uszer was not Russian but Polish in origin and citizenship. He was living in Belgium rather than France after exclusion from Britain. He moved back to Belgium in 1946 and not 1950. Steffi only travelled to meet Uszer twice, not annually.

The file showed that Steffi underwent two extensive and probing interviews with officers from Special Branch following her two applications – mostly about her commitment to Britain, her political views, and her financial probity. The report of the first interview was largely positive. Steffi was described as of good character and uninvolved in communist activity. The second report included some material from the earlier failed application but was much less favourable, concentrating on her assumed continuing communist beliefs and association with communist activists. This was an aspect of her life, it was suggested, that she was reluctant to admit. MI5 showed substantial interest in Steffi's case and, as we can see below, substantial efforts were made to ensure that the service would be consulted at all stages in the application.

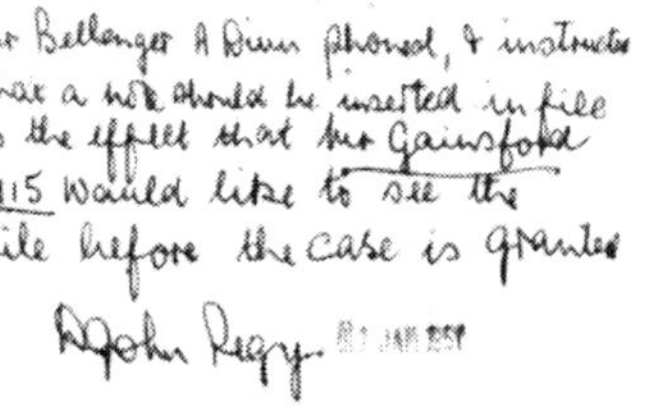

[handwritten note]
Mr Bellenger & Dunn phoned, & instructs that a note should be inserted in file to the effect that Mr Gainsford MI5 would like to see the file before the case is granted

John Legg.

Several unnamed 'sources' affirmed Steffi's continuing communist sympathies. Eventually, it was concluded that, while Steffi did not pose a great security danger, her record of communist sympathies mitigated against her naturalisation 'on security grounds'. An MI5 report stamped confidential and dated 14 June 1955 summarised the case as follows:

> In our earlier assessment of FROCHT dated 3rd April 1951 we drew attention to the fact that the part played by her in the affairs of the war-time "Austrian Centre" left a certain element of doubt regarding her Communist connections and sympathies at that time. In view of this we made further enquiries in July, 1954 from the source referred to in the third paragraph of our earlier assessment to who the applicant is known personally. It was reported as a result of these enquiries that while the applicant was not known to be a member of any Communist Party and did not seem in any way politically active, she was still

unchanged in her sympathies with the Communists, her present political outlook being described as that of a fellow traveller...

We are prepared to believe that the applicant is not fully in agreement with Communist ideology or policy, and we consider that some doubts must still remain as to the extent that she came under the influence of war-time Communist officials at the 'Austrian Centre'. On the basis of what we know about her war-time Communist associations alone, we would not be prepared to recommend refusal of her present application. However, her record since the war in our view leaves no doubt as to the fact that her attitude towards Communism is at least one of sympathetic tolerance. On these grounds therefore while we do not consider that Stephanie FROCHT at present represents a danger to security, we feel justified in recommending refusal of this application for security reasons.

A further note dated 2 September 1955 from the undersecretary of the Home Office, Arthur Samuel, first Baron Bancroft (as it happens also Jewish) approved MI5's recommendation in the interests of the state:

I think that the present circumstances are fairly compared with those when the previous application was turned down... It would be fair to say that this is a borderline case, but on the principle that in such cases the State and not the applicant must have the benefit of the doubt, I agree that this case falls to be refused.

So Steffi's fate rested largely on an unknown source, known to her personally, who had confirmed she was a communist sympathiser. However, such views were never part of her vocabulary or values to my knowledge, and I knew her political views very well. As a family, we talked a lot about politics. Our family was certainly determinedly pro-Labour, with Trude and John very active in local politics in Stoke Newington in the 1950s and 1960s, as was the next generation. Always a strong Labour supporter, though her alien status meant that she could not vote, Steffi never expressed communist sympathies to me and was indeed highly critical of the organisation of the British Communist Party into what she called secretive 'cells'. One must assume that the false picture of her by the MI5 plant was created out of malice, ignorance, or prejudice, if not all of these.

I do not know how my mother felt about the failure of each of her applications and how she responded. I was eleven years old at the time of the second rejection and was probably old enough to appreciate what such a setback might mean. However, she never shared her feelings or disappointments with me. Neither was she given any reason for the failure of her applications. As her file shows, she was inclined to blame Uszer's Belgian family, in particular his wife, Ruchla, for supplying damaging information to the British authorities to prevent his return to the United Kingdom. Uszer, in the usual way he had of riding the waves of controversy, allowed my mother to retain such mistaken opinions about his Belgian wife.

Life went on despite these setbacks. Steffi reverted to her original Austrian citizenship in 1963 as a preliminary to applying for an Austrian restitution pension, and at the same time, she renewed her Austrian passport. This was used only once, a year before she died, to travel to the United States for the wedding of Freda, Tilda's daughter. This trip in 1968 gave her the opportunity of seeing her last remaining sister for the first time in many years. By all accounts, she was made very welcome and found America fascinating, though she laid blame on the fierce air conditioning for the heavy cold that she caught while out there. Interestingly and unbeknown to her, in the same year, her security classification was downgraded from 'secret' to 'confidential', denoting perhaps the fading influence of the Cold War and consequent reduced fear of the spread of communism in Britain.

To my mind, many of the allegations in my mother's file were ill-founded, for example, the extent of her security risk and her supposed commitment to communism. She was always broadly social democratic in belief rather than doctrinaire. But she was, to some extent, naive, seeming to lack understanding of the implications of wartime and Cold War policies and politics on her own life. She also persisted in strong emotional attachments to unappreciative individuals, for example, my father, whom she sought to support and protect whatever the costs to her.

Like most migrants, the three sisters had no option but to work more or less until they dropped, despite their growing frailty. As already stated, they sought office work as their English improved, often working in immigrant or family businesses and organisations known to them. For example, Steffi was employed as a bookkeeper for Trude's husband John for many years until his import/export business folded and, from then, for Fanny's son-in-law, Gerald, who was a chartered accountant. After she reached the official retirement age of sixty, she sought part-time work to boost her British 'old age' pension and the small Austrian 'restitution' pension she had received since 1964. My impression is that she relished the involvement and sociability of 'going out to work', as she put it. By then, her daughter was off her hands so she took the post of part-time administrator for a nursing agency for a further five years until 1968, despite increasing ill health.

In fact, the three sisters were dogged by illness from their arrival in Britain onwards. In her late thirties Steffi was diagnosed with oedema (fluid retention), a potential indicator of a heart condition. Additionally, the serious tram accident when she was evacuated to Leeds late in 1944 left her with limited physical movement. Elsa had lifelong poor eyesight and an early heart condition. Trude was undersized and frail for most of her life. Elsa was the first to go, suffering from a heart attack in June 1962. Trude died four years later in October 1966, also of heart attack. Steffi died of a stroke three years after that, in September 1969. Perhaps immigrant life in the United States in the post-war period was less harsh, since Tilda, the fourth Dinger sister, lived the longest. Following the birth of her daughter Freda in 1946, the death of her first (Austrian) husband in 1955 (in an industrial accident) and remarriage, she died at age ninety-three in November 2002.

Trude was the most politically active of the sisters in Britain, becoming a Labour councillor in Stoke Newington in London along with her Viennese-born husband, John. She was also a noted early campaigner for cervical smear tests for women. That said, in the 1940s and early 1950s, all three sisters were politically engaged and left leaning, in line with much of the country at the time.

How can one summarise a life like that of my mother's? Certainly much went wrong. She faced imminent starvation in the 1914–18 conflict. She endured the rise of the Nazis and, pursuantly, persecution, exile, and the unwarranted deaths of close family members. She had an unsuitable long-term liaison and met rejection of her British citizenship applications, and so on. However, there was much to be grateful for, as my mother would have been the first to admit. She gave thanks for close and loving family relationships, being Jewish, support from unlikely places, establishing roots in a new country, having a child and then grandchildren, and realising a future.

In terms of the relationship of Steffi and Uszer to the security services in the post-war and Cold War periods, they were to some extent treated with care if not with justice. Uszer was an illegal immigrant and communist with a family in Belgium. He was neither destitute nor without a place to go and, therefore, could be rendered a persona non grata without too much difficulty. Steffi was allowed to remain in Britain permanently, and perhaps her rejected naturalisation applications were a small price to pay for having an illegitimate child with an undesirable alien in a foreign land.

What remains disturbing about Steffi's story is the lengths that the security services and, in particular, MI5 were prepared to go and the resources they were prepared to devote to deny an ordinary woman British citizenship, even though she was never judged a risk to security. The employment of secrecy meant that errors were never identified and, therefore, never corrected. It is noticeable in Steffi's Home Office file that, as the story was repeated and embellished by succeeding individuals and groups of civil servants, all of them men, the lies and elaborations came to assume a form of truth that was difficult to challenge.

In hindsight, I am thankful that Steffi never learnt about the reasons for the rejection of her naturalisation applications. The last fifteen years of her life were relatively stable and mainly happy, although as a rebellious adolescent, I was the source of much grief and anxiety in her later life –according to letters to her sister in America and her friends. Steffi and her remaining family were safe, she was able to buy a property and live modestly, and she survived to see two grandchildren and the next generation putting down roots for the future. While it was not, perhaps, the end that she might have envisaged at the start of her life's journey, it was certainly more than she could ever have hoped for in the darkest period of her life. 'Normality', arguably, was her greatest achievement of all.

CHAPTER 13

The Letter, 1963

'We are decent people; only we had to pay a very high price, not to hurt the other people concerned.'

This line comes from a letter sent by my mother to my fiancé prior to our marriage in 1963. In the missive, she disclosed the fact that she and my father were not married and that I was illegitimate – the basis of the elaborate attempts at subterfuge on the day of the wedding. I learnt of the existence of the letter only recently when embarking on research into my family's history and long after my mother's death in 1969. I have only lately seen the original. Written some twenty years after they met in the mid-1940s, this biographical fragment tells of how my parents met, what it was like to be refugees from Nazism who did not know what had happened to their families, and what it meant to bring an illegitimate child into the world at that time. In only three small closely written pages, the letter manages to convey the drama of the time and the reasons why actions were or were not taken. It also illustrates the central tenets of my mother's life – taking responsibility and achieving respectability.

Although I knew of its existence and was promised and expected any day to receive the letter, it was still a shock to see my mother's handwriting and to learn, for the first time from her own hand, the story of her meeting with my father and why they had never married nor indeed lived with each other for any length of time. Because she did not want me to know of my illegitimacy, my mother avoided talking to me about the background to her relationship with my father, and she died before I got round to asking awkward questions. What struck me most of all in rereading the letter is how, in such a short space, she so evocatively captures the choreography of our small family and the complicated manoeuvring of our shared and divided lives – which in various ways I have tried to narrate throughout this book.

At the time of the letter, Steffi was well settled in her own home and, with improving English and a good head for figures, had found regular employment as a bookkeeper. She had raised her daughter almost single-handedly –with some help from her sisters – and had encouraged her to do well at school. Although initially having university ambitions for her, she was pleased to see her difficult and rebellious daughter 'settle down' with someone of whom she approved. He was Jewish, respectable, employed, and on the left politically – although I am not sure if, in the end, the last point was so important to her.

The letter was handwritten on headed notepaper and undated, but it must have been sent before 23 March 1963, the date of the wedding (see full transcript at the end of this chapter). It starts with apologies for not having informed her prospective son-in-law earlier about a matter that might be of some importance to him.

She continues with the excuse that she had not approached him because she had *forgotten* that she was unmarried. She gives as a reason for why she had not revealed her marital circumstances to her daughter, Gaby's presumed 'inferiority complex'. Derived from the work of Austrian psychologists Sigmund Freud and Alfred Adler and used to indicate lack of self-worth and feelings of not quite measuring up to required standards, the concept of *inferiority complex* was popular in the 1950s and 1960s. At the time, it was viewed as originating in the subconscious and characterised either by spectacular achievement or extreme antisocial behaviour, neither of which I displayed. I have no particular memory of feeling inferior, although I had the usual teenage concerns about body image, and I would have preferred not to have a foreign-sounding name. On the contrary, I was lively, sociable, and questioning – so an inferiority complex is something my adult self does not recognise as part of my history. But perhaps my rebellious teenage behaviour gave some indication of insecurity, which became a convenient excuse for my mother not to 'upset' me further.

She states that 'of course' she had to enlighten my fiancé but that, if it made no difference to him, 'you will have no reason whatsoever to be ashamed of me or Eddie'. She describes wartime as a topsy-turvy period. They had met and fallen in love, and not knowing what had happened to their respective families, they'd started a life together and had a daughter. However, when war ended, Eddi had found that his Belgian family was alive and felt compelled to visit them to assess their situation. When Eddi was excluded from Britain, she says, she and he continued to be close, but they also inevitably experienced heartache and disappointment. She had not spoken to her daughter because she was a 'proud' girl, and was afraid she would take news of the illegitimacy badly. Predominantly, the concern in the letter is to convince her future son-in-law of his mother-in-law's respectability and decency and, presumably, his future wife's too:

> I consider myself to be a respectable and responsible person and have tried very hard to bring Gaby up, giving her all my love and attention and unprejudiced advice.

145

We are decent people.

As a new comer to post-war British society, Steffi was well aware of the migrant's need to acquire a reputation for respectability, hard work, and independence. She laboured long and hard to achieve such a status, though she was aware of the dangers, as a non-naturalised citizen, of any reputation for irregularity or dishonour. After all, as we have seen, her partner had been thrown out of Britain for having just such a reputation. The status she sought most mirrored that of a *worthy widow*, and she behaved like one – devoted and reliable. Her status as *mother* likewise gave her permission to hide the truth from her daughter on the grounds of motherly protection and her own acceptance of the situation:'

> I am happy and contented but I was always worried
> how Gaby will take it should she ever know.

The narrative of confusion and turmoil (termed 'topsy-turvy') and conventional love story are fused to provide a rationalisation for why and how hitherto acceptable principles and behaviour were overturned and transformed:

> We became very friendly and gradually meant
> everything to each other. – We did not know what
> tomorrow will bring and decided to live together until
> the time we would be able to marry.

This wartime narrative – of people living for the day because of not knowing what the future might bring – is familiar, and in this respect, Steffi's account is persuasive. The letter evokes a romantic and conventional narrative of excitement – 'no dull moment' – and everlasting if thwarted love.

> Since this time we are more close to each other
> than ever but of course it is a life with heartache,

disappointment, hopes raised, and disillusions and with no dull moment.

This narrative is predominant despite considerable evidence that, at the end of the war, her beloved, whom others have described as somewhat of a charmer and wastrel, settled for the more secure conditions of his first family in Belgium (supported by a factory owning brother-in-law and other in-laws in the diamond business), rather than the more 'immigrant' and marginal life of Steffi and his youngest child.

The letter also utilises a discourse of suffering and sacrifice, not only due to exile and separation but also in terms of the need for secrecy. They decided that their relationship and the existence of their child were to be kept secret from his Belgian family and that their daughter's illegitimacy was to be kept secret, as far as was possible, in order to prevent 'hurt': 'Only we had to pay a very high price, not to hurt the other people concerned'. 'Not hurting people' thus may be seen here as a justification for keeping their relationship beyond scrutiny, yet eternally romantic and permissible.

The central truths conveyed in the letter are the life-lasting love between Steffi and Edi; a mother's care, love, and protection of a vulnerable daughter; and a concern not to hurt others, presumably Edi's wife and the Belgian family. Moreover, as with other autobiographical accounts, Steffi sought to control the narrative. By swearing the receiver of the letter to secrecy and implying that, if he revealed the truth, his future married life might be imperilled, Steffi saw to it that no one could challenge her interpretation of events. What she could not anticipate was her son-in-law Philip's response. Her disclosure, which must have taken much courage and weeks of planning to carry out, meant so little to him that he mislaid the letter among his papers and forgot about its contents until way beyond Steffi's death and his divorce, that is, until searches into family history revealed its existence.

At the time of its writing in 1963, the response to the letter was muted. Presumably there was some small acknowledgement between the receiver and sender – a few words exchanged at a private moment. The receiver adhered to the wishes of the letter writer. The main subject of the letter remained in ignorance, and the matter was lost for decades until the death of the author, Steffi, in 1969. It was then that I learned of my illegitimacy, when I was going through correspondence between Steffi and her friends and family about my birth and seeing these letters for the first time. A question to Fanny Isenstein when I was sitting shiva[107] after my mother's death resulted in confirmation that this was, indeed, the case and a look of considerable surprise that I had not known.

Initially, my newly assumed status of illegitimacy felt colourful and risqué and of little consequence to someone of my generation living through London's Swinging Sixties. However, later and more hurtful, was recognition of the veneer of lies that was needed to sustain the subterfuge. A further personal impact was felt when the letter finally came into my possession early in 2012. Written in my mother's hand, it conveyed a sense of catharsis (of a story finally told), as well as sadness and loss. And in me, it conveyed a sense of the imposed naivety on my younger self, which I have sought to express in my earlier chapter on the wedding. For anyone else, the letter might be interesting as an historical artefact, which provides a glimpse into hitherto unidentified lives, perspectives, and values.

Family discourses, as well as my own memory, indicate that Steffi was a strong and popular woman, a central figure in a small London immigrant family, bright, quick to learn, and hugely grateful for a second chance of life. As with many migrants, she made a success of her life despite many setbacks – exile from home and loss of wider family, physical disability, failure of the relationship with her partner, single parenthood, rejected citizenship applications, and so on. Yet she prospered. She imagined a better life and achieved it. She schemed and strategised. She created alternative truths, which she came to live by. She was able to build strong if flawed relationships. She survived. This is but one migrant story, but it clearly resonates with many others.

The letter is perhaps best in illuminating the values of society of the time (the 1960s) in the particular stratum of society inhabited by 'ordinary' Jewish immigrants from Nazi Europe. Many such Jews gathered in North London in the 1930s, though they gradually dispersed from the 1950s as they became more 'integrated' into British society. Here, and among non-immigrant Londoners, acceptance was denoted (as now) by invisibility in the sense of 'not rocking the boat', 'fitting in', being financially independent, speaking English, and so on. Steffi managed all of this with one exception – her relationship with Edi/Uszer. This, particularly his illegal alien status and the unflinching political views that led to his expulsion and her unsuccessful attempts to become a British citizen, was her vulnerable point. Most difficult of all was his failure to acknowledge openly and take responsibility for his London family. It is this failure and her response to it that makes the letter so fascinating and so poignant.

But why write a letter in the first place? Couldn't my mother have talked to her prospective son-in-law instead? By writing the letter, she perhaps felt that she would be able to take fuller control of the narrative and give greater emphasis to what she perceived were its two predominant elements – lifelong loves (of partner and daughter) and concern not to hurt others. Ostensibly written from the heart, it was also governed by the head, with fate and altruism evoked to defend actions that, to some, might seem indefensible. At the time of its writing, impact was minimal as we have seen, and it is only recently, when its contents have been made public, that the letter has assumed certainly personal but also cultural and historical importance (a version of this chapter was published in 2013)[108]. Did Steffi write the letter because, given her struggles with the English language, she could better express what she wanted to say in written form, with perhaps a dictionary by her side? Certainly, words such as *unprejudiced* and *melodramatic* strike a somewhat artificial note. Or was it that she wanted her side of the story to be told, if not in the1960s to her immediate family, then to future generations?

149

Why was it so difficult for Steffi to tell her eighteen-year-old daughter about her illegitimate status? This was, after all, London in the 1960s, when all sorts of taboos were being overturned and where illegitimacy was no longer such a stigma, at least judging by the relaxed response to the letter from Gaby's fiancé. Perhaps, for Steffi's older generation, illegitimacy continued to be highly stigmatised. Or perhaps a secret so long held could not be easily given up. Or was it that maintaining secrecy preserved the mother's authority over the child?

Finally, might the disclosure of the existence of the letter and this chapter's discussion, be seen, partly at least, as the personal revenge of a daughter at being kept in ignorance for so long? In bringing the letter into the public domain and in questioning its contents, might I, as daughter, be viewed as having turned the tables on my mother, in subverting both the message of the letter and the telling of the story? Perhaps Freud, a contemporary of my mother and also from Vienna, might have had something to say about that.

AFTERWORD: A DIALOGUE
WITH THE DEAD

I have tried in this book to tell my family story and, at the same time, to show the complexity involved in exploring the lives of my mother and other members of my family and the difficulties I had in creating a coherent whole. Eventually, I decided to build the storyline around the lives of three people – my maternal grandmother, Amalia, whom I knew not at all; my father, Uszer, whom I knew only intermittently; and my mother, Steffi, whom I thought I knew very well. All of them died long ago (in 1942, 1980, and 1966 respectively) and, therefore, were not present to inform the content, respond to what has been written, or comment on how they have been portrayed. A fitting way to end this book, therefore, is to create an imaginary dialogue with them and to envisage their responses to the text, their portrayal therein, and what they might think of me as author of their lives.

Amalia, my maternal grandmother, lived the furthest back in time of the three. She was born in mid-Victorian times in a shtctl town in the far east of the Austro-Hungarian Empire, and her life was ended in 1942 in the death camp of Treblinka. What might she have thought of my portrayal of her and the rest of her family? Would she have considered me brave and persistent in seeking out the truth or foolish, ungodly, and trivial? Her struggle to combine modernity with the preservation of her religious and ethnic identity as Jewish in times of deprivation and bigotry, as well as her eventual achievement of relative prosperity out of hardship, might indicate an orientation towards practical action rather than 'bookishness'. Perhaps, given what happened to her, she would, like my father's Belgian family, castigate me for not working to achieve a more secure position for the Jewish people, in a world where anti-Semitism is never far away. Accounts of the past, she might say, are useful in reminding people about the perils of ideological conviction, authoritarianism in governments, and dangerous populist responses to deprivation and dispossession. But are they enough?

Amalia might posit that actions speak louder than words or point to recent failures in Europe and elsewhere to deal with other mass migrations from horror. Perhaps my recent involvement in local politics would impress her more. She would no doubt be proud that aspects of her family life, however inadequately grasped, have been deemed of sufficient interest to be written down and read by a wider public. She would have been delighted that so many of her children survived out of the horror of Nazism and that they were able to create new lives for themselves and new families. She would have been saddened that this had to take place elsewhere than in her beloved Vienna. She would perhaps have been shocked at some of the unorthodox emotional attachments and relationships of her daughters and grandchildren but aware also that each generation has to make its own future, as she and her husband David sought to do so long ago, in moving their burgeoning family from Brody to Vienna.

Uszer, my father, on the other hand, would be more 'knowing' about what I have been trying to do and more aware of the different strands that I have sought to incorporate in producing a credible narrative. Lacking formal education, but multilingual, politically astute, and curious, he would have been pleased to see his youngest daughter taking on the wider movements of history in explaining the 'why' and the 'how', as well as the 'what' of bygone events that impacted on his individual family members. He never repudiated the Marxism of his youth and died a decade before the Berlin Wall came down and the Soviet Union collapsed. However, as far as I can remember, he was never doctrinaire, just rather too optimistic that his particular brand of politics could deliver a better world. He was aware when we met in the 1960s and 1970s of my orientation towards left-leaning politics and, in particular, feminism, with which he had less sympathy.

I imagine, though, that he would be pleased with the book overall and interested in the story of Amalia, because such stories ensure, as he wrote to me, that we 'Never forget'. He would also be fascinated by the extent of the surveillance of my mother and MI5's interest in him in the 1950s but not surprised. He was under no illusion about the opposition communism attracted throughout the twentieth century. Neither did he underestimate the efforts made by governments and officials to keep it in check when and where possible. While he might challenge the accuracy of my account about aspects of his own life, he would be spellbound by the contents of his Brussels' file and would no doubt want to read it in full. Again, the contents of the file would not have surprised him, as he was always aware of the potential danger of his political viewpoints and actions – though the documentation on his expulsion from Belgium might have filled in some gaps for him on the sequence of events leading to it.

He might even be somewhat shamefaced about his evident duplicity in promising my mother that he was seeking a divorce from his wife at the same time as making every effort to rejoin his first family and ensure permanent residence in Belgium. But he was always a charmer and no doubt would have explained it all away. Given his own track record of difficult relationships and unintended outcomes, he would have been less judgemental than others of his generation about the unconventional and broken relationships of those following. He referred to his own wife and family in Belgium as *petit bourgeois* in a conversation with me in the early 1970s, to justify why he had not told them of the existence of my mother and me. Might he give the same label to me in writing this book?

The person, however, who I imagine would be most disturbed by the book is my mother Steffi, who was the original central focus of my investigation. As already noted, I initially wanted to find out more about how she and her sisters had come to Britain, particularly because they had no particular influence or wealth. I anticipated that their story would differ from other Austrian refugees from more privileged backgrounds who have written or have had written books about their experiences. I was interested in the Dinger sisters as 'ordinary' women, as with a few exceptions, history tends to view ordinariness as dreary and of little import. A close focus on individuals, however superficially non-remarkable, inevitably lifts them out of obscurity and renders them, to some extent, exceptional. And there is no doubt that Steffi would relish that perception of herself and her sisters. She would be pleased to see the attention paid to her beloved mother, although deeply saddened (yet again) by the manner of Amalia's death.

Had she been alive, Steffi would be able to provide more detail of her own life in Vienna, as a child and young adult, and of her fiancé in Vienna and what he'd meant to her. She would have remembered the events leading up to the Anschluss and the aftermath – though it must be said that she was always reluctant to talk about this period. She would also be able to provide the detail of her escape, the documents needed, the people she had to see, the details of her journey to England, and so on.

She would be less happy with the description of her relationship with Uszer, the doubts raised about his intentions towards her, and the discussion surrounding my birth. She would be horrified by the appearance of her daughter's illegitimacy in her National Archive documentation and her consequent treatment by the officials dealing with her case. As she wrote to her prospective son-in-law, she had made every effort to 'forget' that she was not married. She would be even more disturbed by the account of the wedding in 1963 and the retrospective humiliation felt by her daughter, in being among the few present who did not know of her illegitimate status. How might she have sought to defend her actions, if not on paper, as in the letter to her prospective son-in-law, then in person to her daughter? Would she have echoed her claim to be protecting the vulnerable? Surely not, if Steffi deemed her eighteen-year-old daughter mature and independent enough to get married. Might she be prepared to admit that the main reason for keeping the illegitimacy secret was her concern not to pierce the veneer of respectability and propriety that she had struggled so hard to create in building a life for her and her daughter in London?

She would also probably be dismayed by the attention given to the letter to her future son-in-law, the speculation concerning why it was written, and the fact that the illegitimacy was at last public – some sixty years after the event. Would she have minded at this late stage, now that her cousin Fanny and her contemporaries were all long gone? For me, writing about the letter assumed importance mainly because it generated and exonerated feelings of foolishness at having been deliberately kept ignorant. Would she have apologised or, instead, accused me of deliberately making public something that she so clearly wanted kept quiet.

Finally, Steffi would be astonished by the revelations in her National Archive file that the reason for the rejection of her naturalisation applications was due to Uszer's politics and her own commitment to keeping the relationship with him going rather than any vendetta, as she supposed, on the part of Uszer's wife. The Belgian file's disclosure of Uszer's frantic efforts to get back to Belgium and to his first family in 1946, despite his declared commitment to staying in London, would also be a shock. I suspect that she would make some excuse or other for him, as she was soft-hearted and trusting and loved him dearly despite his evident faults. Also, not having him in the background would have spoiled the careful choreography surrounding the performance of her life.

And having completed the book, what can I say in conclusion? First, this has been a project that has lasted for nearly a decade, and I am relieved now to have completed it. I am delighted to have been able to find out so much about the three lives, but have frequently been jolted by the wave of revelations along the way. Among these were Uszer's flight from Polish military service; the confirmation of the existence of 'the letter'; the secrecy built around the illegitimacy; the level of surveillance undertaken by the British Security Service in the 1950s; and perhaps, most of all, the struggle that I had to get access to my mother's file. I have pondered long and hard on the role of the security forces and their treatment of refugees such as my mother and father.

My mother's failure to gain naturalisation, which at the time was believed to be unjust and undeserved, ultimately yielded a bonus in terms of the records preserved that would otherwise have been destroyed. Not only did it include important information about her life, but it also provided an exemplar of how British civil servants carried out their business at the height of the Cold War. Mostly, civil servants were suspicious of the motives of migrants and quick to jump to the most negative conclusions about what they might bring, economically and politically, to Britain. Also while joined-up policy implementation was an aspiration between Jewish voluntary organisations, police, special branch, passport control, MI5, and so on, errors were made, and prejudices were exercised that were not challengeable because they were made in secret.

My mother's documents reveal a clear demarcation between the reports on civilians (citizens) that were open to the people involved (for example, registration documents) and those that were not (such as comments on suitability to enter Britain or for British citizenship). Given that the 1940s and 1950s were periods of global warfare and political hostility, the practice of secrecy is not surprising. What is surprising is the inaccessibility of such documentation *today*, notwithstanding the recent Freedom of Information legislation (2000). Steffi's file was original closed until 2069, and the date for open access is now put at 2046 – more than a century after my birth. At present, as her only child and because I am mentioned in it, I am the only person allowed to see the file in its entirety, excepting a few redacted names. I struggled to gain access to this information, which should be in the public record, and am still denied information relating to named people (of those similarly under scrutiny or of informers), all long dead. Who, I want to ask, is protecting whom and for what reasons? How might the rights of family and individuals, as well as historians, to know about the past be judged against, in this case, the outdated interests of the state? Or is there something else we have not been told?

I have also been made aware that refugees like my mother, her sisters, and my father who were accepted, however reluctantly, into Britain, the United States, France, Belgium, Palestine, and so on, were the lucky ones. Those who were refused mostly died. Bureaucracies placed on a war footing acted in favour of the state rather than the individual. Against this background, it was considered that any minor harassment perpetrated against incomers or any restriction of their rights was the price they had to pay for the right to life. And indeed this is largely how my mother and her sisters understood their reception in Britain.

State self-interest was clearly balanced against humanitarian concern in the British response to the plight of European Jews at the onset of Nazism, as shown by Louise London, in her study of the treatment of Jews by British government officials between 1933 and 1948.[109] While some working at Whitehall and in the secret services were compassionate and had genuine concerns about the fate of European Jews, British self-interest consistently sought to limit immigration and the economic cost of refugees – a policy stance visible in my mother's case too. It was judged that she and her two younger sisters, rather than her older sister, younger brother, mother, or aunt, would be most beneficial to the British economy. Decisions about who should be allowed entry were pragmatic and sometimes random. British officials, for example, categorised Czech Jews as 'economic refugees', as opposed to Germans who were adjudged 'political refugees,' more vulnerable to persecution and therefore more deserving of rescue. They rejected the very old and the very young, men more than women, and those who were seen as likely to be a burden on the state or who might take jobs from British workers or professionals. Refugee agencies also played their parts in choosing who should be admitted; 'Anglo-Jewish leaders favoured German Jews over Austrians and declined responsibility for Jews from Czechoslovakia'.[110] There was also the long-term fear, expressed by both government and refugee agencies, that acceptance of too many of the 'wrong' Jews would lead to an explosion of British anti-Semitism that might be difficult to control. One outcome of this exploration, thus, has been an insight into governmental responses to the needs of the dispossessed and persecuted, responses that are very evident today.

Finally, it is important to restate that this has not been a story of conventional achievement. Nor is it about identifying heroes and heroines. Nevertheless, as my investigation comes to an end, I feel proud to be associated with the three people whose lives I have sought to narrate. They did their best in circumstances not of their own choosing and lived commendable and principled, if not always virtuous, lives. Whether they would see their portrayals as accurate or even recognisable is something that we shall never know. But, as my mother said to me on many occasions, 'You can only do your best.' Throughout the ups and downs of this study of lives, that is what I have aspired to do.

Transcript of letter from Steffi Frocht to Philip Weiner

The letter, on headed notepaper with the address given as 48 Gloucester Drive, London N4, and telephone number as Stamford Hill 9466, is undated but was sent from Steffi Frocht to Philip Weiner before 23 March 1963, the day of his marriage to Steffi's daughter, Gaby. Small errors of expression, grammar and punctuation have been left in the original. Interestingly, Steffi refers to Eddi, rather than Edi as he was known in London and as he used in his signature.

Dear Phillip

I think I should have informed you earlier about my own state of affairs, which might be important to you. I have almost forgotten that I am not married to Gaby's Father, as I have so much rejected the idea and have buried the whole matter inside me so completely, that it takes sometimes time to remember it. Gaby is unaware of it and the reason why I never told her is the following:

1.) She suffered so much under an inferiority complex, that it would have been cruel to add more to her lot.

2.) Children speak freely and for her sake and my own I did not want to be a target for gossip and sneer.

I consider myself to be a respectable and responsible person and have tried very hard to bring Gaby up, giving her all my love and attention and unprejudiced advice. She in return has given me a lot of happiness for which I thank her with all my heart. Why I did not marry Gaby's father is rather, seen today, melodramatic. It was during the war the World was topsy turvy. My family which were all left behind were threatened with Gas Chambers etc. and Eddi held a Service for the Jewish people under Hitler – so we met. We became very friendly and gradually meant everything to each other. – We did not know what tomorrow will bring and decided to live together until the time we would be able to marry. Eddi did not live with his family before he came to England and friend told him, that his family is sharing the same fate as all other Jewish people under Hitler. But his family was lucky to escape and when Gaby was already on the way we heard the News that his family has escaped the Gas Chambers. After the war, I persuaded him to go back and see what he could do to help. – He returned and told me, that he cannot live with his family, his place is with me but he has once more to go home, as he has applied for a pension, which he had intended to transfer to his family. – However on his second arrival he was given 3 months to leave the country. Since this time we are more close to each other than ever but of course it is a life with heartache, disappointment, hopes raised, and disillusions and with no dull moment. I am happy and contented but I was always worried how Gaby will take it should she ever know. I cannot make up my mind whether to talk to her or not and I leave things at the moment as they are. – Gaby is a very proud girl and I do not want to hurt her feelings, nor do I want her to resent me for it. –

But of course, I had to tell you and if it makes no difference to you, I promise you you will have no reason whatsoever to be ashamed of me or Eddie. We are decent people, only we had to pay a very high price, not to hurt the other people concerned. Please do not tell anyone without my knowledge and not Gaby of all people.

I do know you enough to trust you in this matter.

Love Steffi Frocht

ABOUT THE AUTHOR

Gaby Weiner has worked at various universities in the United Kingdom and Sweden and is currently Visiting Research Professor at Sussex University and Professorial Research Fellow at Manchester Metropolitan University. She has written and edited a number of academic publications, in particular on gender and social justice in education. This volume, however, on the lives of her maternal grandmother and mother and father, is a new venture for her and has taken her nearly a decade to complete. She has lived most of her life in the United Kingdom, although she spent some years in Sweden in the early 2000s. This book is for her children, grandchildren, extended family members, and the wider reading public.

BIBLIOGRAPHY

Ackerman, Karen, *The Night Crossing* (Random House. USA: Children's Books, 1995).

Andrew, Christopher, *The Defence of the Realm: The Authorized History of MI5* (London: Penguin Books, 2010).

Baranowski, Julian Litzmannstadt Ghetto 1940–1944, in Andrzej Machejek (ed.), *Jews of Lodz* (Lodz, Poland: Wydawnictwo Hamal, 2009), 85–1,001.

Bauer-Manhart, Inger, *Jewish Vienna – Heritage and Mission* (Vienna: Vienna City Administration, 2010).

Bearman, Marietta, Brinson, Charmian, Dove, Richard, Grenville, Anthony, and Taylor, Jennifer (eds.), *Out of Austria: The Austrian Centre in London in World War II* (London: Tauris Academic Books, 2008).

Brinson, Charmian, 'A Woman's Place…? German-Speaking Women in Exile in Britain 1933–45', in Deborah Vietor-Engländer (ed.), *The Legacy of Exile: Lives, Letters, Literature*. (London: Blackwell, 1998), 54–74.

——, 'The "Robinson Crusoes of Paddington": Relations between the Free Austrians and their British Hosts', in Marietta Bearman, Charmian Brinson, Richard Dove, Anthony Grenville, and

Jennifer Taylor (eds.), *Out of Austria: The Austrian Centre in London in World War II* (London: Tauris Academic Books, 2008), 175–209.

—— and Dove, Richard, 'Free Austrian Books: The Austrian Centre and its Publications 1939–1946', in Ian Wallace (ed.), *German Speaking Exiles in Great Britain* (Amsterdam: Rodopi, 1999), 219–41.

————, *A Matter of Intelligence: MI5 and the Surveillance of Anti-Nazi Refugees 1933–50* (Manchester: Manchester University Press, 2014).

Buber-Neumann, Margaret, *Under Two Dictators: Prisoner of Stalin and Hitler* (London: Gollancz, 1949).

Clare, George, *Last Waltz in Vienna* (1981; London: Macmillan, 2002 edn.).

Cole, G. D. H. and Postgate, Raymond, *The Common People 1746–1946* (1961; London: Methuen,1987 edn.).

Delaet, Jean-Louis, *Les Charbonnages du pays de Charleroi aux XIXe and XXe siècles*, 2010, http://sites.univ-provence.fr/mines/Geographie/geo_belgique/geo_notice_belgique.htm.

De Waal, Edmund, *The Hare with the Amber Eyes* (London: Vintage Books, 2010).

Elon, Amos, *The Pity of It All: A Portrait of the German-Jewish Epoch 1743–1933* (London: Allen Lane, 2002).

Gedye, G.E.R, *Fallen Bastions: The Central European Tragedy* (London: Victor Gollancz, 1939).

Gilbert, Martin, *Never Again: A History of the Holocaust* (London: HarperCollins*Illustrated*, 2000).

Gildea, Robert, *Fighters in the Shadows: A New History of the French Resistance* (London: Faber & Faber, 2015).

Healy, Maureen, *Vienna and the Fall of the Hapsburg Empire: Total War and Everyday Life in World War I* (Cambridge: Cambridge University Press, 2007).

Hobsbawm, Eric, *The Age of Extremes: The Short Twentieth Century* (London: Michael Joseph, 1994).

——, *Interesting Times: A Twentieth Century Life* (London: Penguin, Allen Lane, 2002).

John, Angela V., *By the Sweat of Their Brow: Women Workers at Victorian Coalmines* (London: Routledge & Kegan Paul, 1984).

Kean, Hilda, *London Stories: Personal Lives, Public Histories* (London: Rivers Oram Press, 2004).

Kerr, Judith, *When Hitler Stole Pink Rabbit* (London: William Collins and Sons, 1971).

——, *Bombs on Aunt Dainty*, (London: William Collins and Sons, 1975).

Koschland, Bernd, 'House of a Thousand Destinies: The Jews' Temporary Shelter', *Association of Jewish Refugees' Newsletter*, August 2014, vol. 14, issue 8, p 3.

London, Louise, *Whitehall and the Jews 1933–1948* (Cambridge: Cambridge University Press, 2000).

Lowry, Lois, *Number the* Stars (1969; Boston: Houghton Mifflin, 2011 edn.).

Lux, Joseph August, *Künstlerische Kodakgeheimnisse* (Artistic Secrets of the Kodak), 1908.

Machejek, Andrzej (ed.), *Jews of Lodz* (Lodz. Poland: Wydawnictwo Hamal, 2009).

Mason, John W., *The Dissolution of the Austro-Hungarian Empire 1867–1918* (London: Longman, 1997).

Morton, A. L., *A People's History of England* (London: Lawrence and Wishart, 1938).

Nadel, Ira Bruce, *Biography: Fiction, Fact & Form* (St Martins Press, 1986).

Pehle, Walther H., 'Editor's Preface', in Walther H. Pehle, (ed.) *From Reichskristall nacht to Genocide* (1938; New York: Berg Publishers Inc., English edn, 1991.)

Pipes, Richard, 'Jews and the Russian Revolution: A Note', in Anton Polonsky, Israel Bartel, Gershon Hundert, Magdalena Opalski, and Jerzy Tomaszewski (eds.), *Polin Studies in Polish Jewry Volume 9: Poles, Jews, Socialists: The Failure of an Ideal* (London: Littman Library of Jewish Civilisation, 1996), 55–7.

Poliakov, Léon, *The History of Anti-Semitism* (Pennsylvania: University of Pennsylvania Press, 2003).

Rathkolb, Oliver, 'The Anschluss in the Rear-View Mirror, 1938–2008: Historical Memories between Debate and Transformation', in Günter Bischof, Fritz Plasser, and Barbara Stelzl-Marx (eds.), *New Perspectives on Austrians and World War II* (New Brunswick, NJ: Transaction Publishers, 2009) 5–28.

Rozenblit, Marsha L., *The Jews of Vienna 1867–1914: Assimilation and Identity* (Albany: SUNY, 1983).

Ross, Henryk, Weber, Thomas, Parr, Martin, and Prus, Timothy, *Lodz Ghetto Album* (New York: Chris Boot: Archive of Modern Conflict, 2005).

Roth, Joseph, *Radetzky March*, trans. Michael Hofmann (1932; London: Granta, 2013 edn.).

——, *The Wandering Jews*, trans. M. Hofmann. (1927; London: Granta, 2001 edn.).

Saerens, Lieven, 'The Attitude of the Belgian Roman Catholic Clergy towards the Jews Prior to the Occupation', in Don Michman (ed.), *Belgium and the Holocaust: Jews, Belgians, Germans* (Jerusalem: Vad Yashem, 1998), 117–57.

Schatz, Jaff, *The Generation* (California: University of California Press, 1991).

Schnur, Steven, *The Shadow Children* (New York: HarperCollins, 1994).

Seller, Maxine S., *We Built Up Our Lives: Education and Community among Jewish Refugees Interned by Britain in World War II* (Westport, CT: Greenwood Press, 2001).

Sereny, Gitta, *The German Trauma: Experiences and Reflections 1938–2000* (London: Allen Lane Penguin, 2000).

Simon, Marie Jalowicz, *Gone to Ground*, trans. Anthea Bell (London: Clerkenwell Press, 2014).

Smith, Mark, *Treblinka Survivor: The Life and Death of Hershl Sperling* (Stroud, England: The History Press, 2010).

Srebnik, Henry Felix, *London Jews and British Communism 1935–1945* (Ilford, Essex, UK: Valentine Mitchell, 1995).

——, 'Birodbidzhan: a Remnant of History', *Jewish Currents* 2, 2012, 16–22, http://jewishcurrents.org/wp-content/uploads/2010/02/Birobidzhan.pdf.

Swindells, Julia, *Victorian Writing and Working Women* (London: Polity Press, 1985).

Szasz, T., *Karl Kraus and the Soul Doctors* (Routledge & Kegan Paul, 1977), quoted in Mason, John W., *The Dissolution of the Austro-Hungarian Empire, 1867–1918* (UK: Longman, 1997 edn.).

Thompson, E. P., *The Making of the English Working Class* (1963; Harmondsworth: Penguin, 1980 edn.).

Troller, Norbert, *Theresienstadt: Hitler's Gift to the Jews* (North Carolina: University of North Carolina Press, 1991).

Van Doorslaer, Rudi, 'Jewish Immigration and Communism in Belgium, 1925–39), in Don Michman (ed.), *Belgium and the Holocaust: Jews, Belgians, Germans* (Jerusalem: Vad Yashem, 1998) 63–83.

Wachsmann, Nikolaus, 'Introduction', in Buber-Neumann, Margaret, *Under Two Dictators: Prisoner of Stalin and Hitler* (1949; revised publication with new introduction, UK: Random House, 2008 edn.), vii–xxii.

Wasserman, Janek, *Black Vienna: The Radical Right in the Red City, 1918–1938* (Ithaca, NY: Cornell University Press, 2014).

Wasserstein, Bernard, *On the Eve: The Jews of Europe before the Second Word War* (London: Profile Books, 2013).

Weiner, Gaby, 'We are decent people; only we had to pay a very high price, not to hurt the other people concerned': Three lives in a letter', in Andrew C. Sparkes (ed.), *Auto/Biography Yearbook 2012* (Durham: Russell Press, 2013), 48–60.

Zamorski, Adam, *The Polish Way: A Thousand-year History of the Poles and their Culture* (London: John Murray, 1987).

ENDNOTES

1   E. P. Thompson, *The Making of the English Working Class* (1963; 3rd edn. London: Victor Gollancz, 1980).

2   Examples of histories of ordinary people taken from my bookshelf include the following works: Hilda Kean, *London Stories: Personal Lives, Public Histories* (London: Rivers Oram Press, 2004); Angela. V. John, *By the Sweat of Their Brow: Women Workers at Victorian Coalmines* (London: Routledge & Kegan Paul, 1984); A. L. Morton, *A People's History of England* (London: Lawrence and Wishart, 1938); G. D. H. Cole and Raymond Postgate, *The Common People 1746–1946* (1961; London: Methuen, 1987 edn.); Julia Swindells, *Victorian Writing and Working Women* (London: Polity Press, 1985).

3   Books about the Holocaust written especially for children include *The Night Crossing* by Karen Ackerman, *The Shadow Children* by Steven Schnur, *Number the Stars* by Lois Lowry, and *When Hitler Stole Pink Rabbit* by Judith Kerr.

4   The Holocaust is the term used for the systematic persecution and murder of approximately six million Jews by the Nazi regime and its collaborators, though other groups are also recognised as Holocaust victims, including Roma and people with disabilities.

5   Henry Felix Srebnik, *London Jews and British Communism 1935–1945* (Ilford, Essex, UK: Valentine Mitchell, 1995), 91.

6   Judith Kerr *Bombs on Aunt Dainty* (HarperCollins, 2002), 108–9.

7   Charmian Brinson and Richard Dove, *A Matter of Intelligence: MI5 and the Surveillance of Anti-Nazi Refugees 1933–50* (Manchester: Manchester University Press, 2014).

8   There are two main meaning of the word *kosher*. Originally, it referred to the food permissible according to traditional Jewish dietary laws. English slang offers another meaning – proper, legitimate, genuine, fair, or acceptable. Here, kosher is used to denote a legitimate Jewish interest.

9   Food prepared according to Jewish dietary laws. See also chapter 1.

10 Boleslaw Kulczycki, 'Genocide in Brody' (published online 1999) <http://kehilalinks.jewishgen.org/brody/boleslaw_kulczycki_memoir.htm> downloaded 18 April 2016

11 'Shtetl', in *The Yivo Encyclopedia* <http://www.yivoencyclopedia.org/article. aspx/Shtetl>

12 Extracted from 'Mission of Inquiry to the Jews of Brody', in *Narrative of a Mission of Inquiry to the Jews from the Church of Scotland in 1839* (Edinburgh: William Whyte & Co, 1844) 1 <http://www.shtetlinks.jewishgen.org/brody/ mission_of_inquiry.htm>, accessed 1 February 2011

13 Joseph Roth, *The Wandering Jews*, trans. Michael Hofmann (1927; London: Granta, 2001 edn.) 6.

14 The Association of Jewish Refugees (AJR) is the principal organisation representing former Jewish refugees from Nazism. It was founded in 1941, and continues until today. Until recently, there has been little academic study of this refugee community. Naturalisation was one of the dominant topics of the early years of AJR. Refugees were enjoined to act as loyal citizens, be grateful for being allowed to stay, and not rock the boat or allow anti-Semitism to emerge.

15 Jewish Telegraph Agency, 'London to Broadcast May First Message to Jewish Workers in Poland', 28 April 1942 <accessed at www.jta.org/london-to-broadcast-may-first-message-to-jewish-worker> accessed 17 February 2016

16 From interview with relative of original organisers.

17 Henry Felix Srebrnik, *London Jews and British Communism 1935–45* (Ilford, Essex: Valentine Mitchell, 1995) 73.

18 Eric Hobsbawm, *The Age of Extremes: The Short Twentieth Century.* (London: Michael Joseph, 1994).

19 The family name was Frokht in Russia, Frocht in Poland, Frucht in Belgium, and Frocht in Britain.

20 Russian census, 1897

21 Andrzej Machejek (ed.), *Jews of Lodz* (Lodz, Poland: Wydawnictwo Hamal Andrzej Machejek, 2009) 12.

22 Adam Zamorski, *The Polish Way: A Thousand-Year History of the Poles and their Culture* (London: John Murray, 1987), 337.

23 Richard Pipes, 'Jews and the Russian Revolution: A Note', in Anton Polonsky, Israel Bartel, Gershon Hundert, Magdalena Opalski, and Jerzy Tomaszewski (eds.) *Polin Studies in Polish Jewry Volume 9: Poles, Jews, Socialists: The Failure of an Ideal* (London: Littman Library of Jewish Civilisation, 1996), 55–7.

24 Jaff Schatz, *The Generation* (University of California Press, 1991).

25 Ibid., 57.

26 Bernard Wasserstein, *On the Eve. The Jews of Europe before the Second Word War* (London: Profile Books, 2013), 176.

27 Robert Gildea, *Fighters in the Shadows: A New History of the French Resistance* (London: Faber & Faber, 2015).

28 This is not strictly true. Uszer did return to Poland, to Auschwitz, near Krakow, in 1967 for a short visit on the opening of the death camp to the public. But this was the only time he went back to Poland.

29 Marsha L. Rozenblit, *The Jews of Vienna 1867–1914: Assimilation and Identity* (Albany: SUNY, 1983).

30 John W. Mason, *The Dissolution of the Austro-Hungarian Empire, 1867–1918* (Longman, 1997).

31 T. Szasz, *Karl Kraus and the Soul Doctors* (Routledge & Kegan Paul, 1977), quoted in Mason, *Dissolution*.

32 G. E. R Gedye, *Fallen Bastions. The Central European Tragedy* (London: Victor Gollancz, 1939), 22.

33 Maureen Healy, *Vienna and the Fall of the Hapsburg Empire: Total War and Everyday Life in World War I* (Cambridge: Cambridge University Press, 2007).

34 Ibid., 3.

35 Ibid., 17.

36 Joseph August Lux, *Künstlerische Kodakgeheimnisse* (Artistic Secrets of the Kodak), 1908.

37 George Clare, *Last Waltz in Vienna* (1981; London: Macmillan, 2002 edn.).

38 Eric Hobsbawm, *Interesting Times: A Twentieth Century Life* (London: Penguin, Allen Lane, 2002), 24.

39 See http://www.fsmitha.com/h2/ch19vienna.html.

40 Amos Elon, *The Pity of It All: A Portrait of the German-Jewish Epoch, 1743–1933,* (London: Allen Lane, 2002), 224.

41 Léon Poliakov, *The History of Anti-Semitism* (University of Pennsylvania Press, 2003), 24.

42 Janek Wasserman, *Black Vienna: The Radical Right in the Red City, 1918–1938* (Cornell University Press, 2014).

43 Clare, *Last Waltz*, 219–20.

44 Ibid., 221.

45 Oliver Rathkolb, 'The Anschluss in the Rear-View Mirror; 1938–2008: Historical Memories between Debate and Transformation', in Günter Bischof, Fritz Plasser, and Barbara Stelzl-Marx (eds.) *New Perspectives on Austrians and World War II* (New Brunswick, NJ: Transaction Publishers, 2009), 12.

46 Pehle writes: 'With good reason, knowledgeable commentators urge people to renounce the continued use of "Kristallnacht" and "Reichskristall-nacht" to refer to these events, even if the expressions have become slick and established usage in our language.' Pehle, W. H., 'Preface', in Pehle, W. H. (ed.), *From Reichskristall nacht to Genocide* (1938; English edn., New York: Berg Publishers Inc., NY, 1991), vii–viii.

47 Maxine S. Seller, *We Built Up Our Lives: Education and Community among Jewish Refugees Interned by Britain in World War II* (Westport Connecticut: Greenwood Press, 2001), 26.

48 The main aim of 'Aryanisation' (in German, Arisierung) was the transfer of Jewish property into 'Aryan' hands in order to make the Nazi economy 'Jew-free'.

49 In 1934, a five-schilling coin was worth fifteen US dollars (from http://www.austriancoins.com/coinvalues.html).

50 In 1938, after Austria's incorporation into the Reich, the currency exchange was 2 German Reichsmark equalled 3 schilling.

51 The date was stamped on their passports

52 Louise London, *Whitehall and the Jews 1933–1948: British Immigration Policy and the Holocaust* (Cambridge: Cambridge University Press, 2000).

53 Minutes of Application for Visa meeting, Aliens Department, Home Office, 18 July 1938, lodged in Steffi's Home Office file.

54 Clare, *Last Waltz*, 242.

55 Unedited full text of 1906 *Jewish Encyclopaedia*, downloaded from http://www.jewishencyclopedia.com/articles/11660-odessa

56 Edmund De Waal, *The Hare with the Amber Eyes* (London: Vintage Books, 2010), 118.

57 Hobsbawm, *Interesting Times*, 22.

58 Rathkolb, 'Anschluss in the Rear-View', 11.

59 Nikolaus Wachsmann, 'Introduction', in Buber-Neumann, Margaret, *Under Two Dictators: Prisoner of Stalin and Hitler* (1949; Pimlico, 2008 edn), vii–xxii.

60 Buber-Neumann, op cit.

61 Supplied by the Archive of the Jewish Community in Vienna, 27 January 2012

62 Record 81, Belgian file, Uszer Frucht

63 Jean-Louis Delaet, *Les Charbonnages du pays de Charleroi aux XIXe and XXe siècles*, 2010, http://sites.univ-provence.fr/mines/Geographie/geo_belgique/geo_notice_belgique.htm.

64 Wasserstein, *On the Eve*, 11.

65 Rudi Van Doorslaer, 'Jewish Immigration and Communism in Belgium, 1925–39', in Don Michman (ed.) *Belgium and the Holocaust: Jews, Belgians, Germans* (Jerusalem: Vad Yashem, 1998) 63-83.

66 Lieven Saerens, 'The Attitude of the Belgian Roman Catholic Clergy towards the Jews Prior to the Occupation', in Don Michman (ed.) *Belgium and the Holocaust: Jews, Belgians, Germans* (Jerusalem: Vad Yashem, 1998), 117–57.

67 Van Doorslaer, 'Jewish Immigration', 71.

Tales of Loving and Leaving

68 Henry Felix Srebrnik 'Birodbidzhan: A Remnant of History', *Jewish Currents* 2, (2012), 16–22. <http://jewishcurrents.org/wp-content/uploads/2010/02/Birobidzhan.pdf.>

69 A small Jewish community was re-established after 1989, following the collapse of the Soviet Union (see for instance, Srebrnik above).

70 Later, *Beaverdale* was one of eighteen of the company's fleet requisitioned for war service by British Admiralty. During wartime, the 'Beaver' vessels were classed as merchant ships with civilian crews. Together they carried over a million tons of cargo and a million troops and civilians across the Atlantic. In April 1941, *Beaverdale* was torpedoed and sunk off the coast of Iceland with the loss of twenty crew members and a gunner. See http://www.uboat.net/allies/merchants/ships/847.html.

71 Administrative record of police statement describing the arrest of Uszer, and an account of Uszer's testimony, translated into English from the original Flemish (record 170, Belgian file, Uszer Frucht)

72 *Kindertransport* is the informal name given to a series of rescue efforts. The exact number of children rescued is unknown, but it is estimated that up to ten thousand Jewish refugee children were brought to Britain from Germany, Austria, Czechoslovakia, Poland, and Danzig in the years 1938 and 1939.

73 Seller, *We Built Up Our Lives*, 51.

74 Interview with John Spencer, Trude's husband (1986)

75 Interview with Amalia (Mali) Michaels, Fanny's older daughter (2009)

76 Ibid.

77 Steffi's Registration Card

78 Marietta Bearman, Charmian Brinson, Richard Dove, Anthony Grenville, and Jennifer Taylor (eds.), *Out of Austria. The Austrian Centre in London in World War II* (London: Tauris Academic Books, 2008).

79 File FO 371/34464, mentioned in Charmian Brinson, 'The "Robinson Crusoes of Paddington": Relations between the Free Austrians and their British Hosts', in Marietta Bearman, Charmian Brinson, Richard Dove, Anthony Grenville, and Jennifer Taylor (eds.), *Out of Austria: The Austrian Centre in London in World War II* (London: Tauris Academic Books, 2008), 175–209, footnote 137.

80 Charmian Brinson and Richard Dove, 'Free Austrian Books: The Austrian Centre and its Publications 1939–1946', in Ian Wallace (ed.), *German Speaking Exiles in Great Britain* (Amsterdam: Rodopi, 1999) 219–41.

81 Message posted on www.gabyweiner.co.uk, from Stephen Elster 31 March 2015

82 Bernd Koschland (2014) House of a Thousand Destinies: The Jews' Temporary Shelter. *Association of Jewish Refugees' Newsletter*. August, vol. 14, issue 8, p.3.

83   For overview of the Jewish Shelter movement, see http://www.jewisheastend. com/shelter.html

84   Interview with John Spencer (1986)

85   Srebrnik, *London Jews and British Communism*, 27.

86   Letter from Fanny Isenstein, dated 14 May 1944

87   Inger Bauer-Manhart, *Jewish Vienna – Heritage and Mission* (Vienna: Vienna City Administration, 2010).

88   Martin Gilbert, *Never Again: A History of the Holocaust* (HarperCollins Illustrated, 2000), 70–1.

89   Marie Jalowicz Simon, *Gone to Ground*, trans. Anthea Bell (London: Clerkenwell Press, 2014).

90   Ibid., 55.

91   Taken from <http://www.deathcamps.org/reinhard/austriatransports.htm>

92   See, for example, <http://www.youtube.com/watch?v=atNum02TPsc>

93   The Gestapo provided political supervision of the ghetto. Kripo, the criminal police, conducted the confiscation of Jewish property. Schupo guarded the ghetto borders. Julian Baranowski, 'Litzmannstadt Ghetto 1940–1944', in Andrzej Machejek (ed.) *Jews of Lodz* (Lodz, Poland: Wydawnictwo Hamal Andrzej Machejek, 2009), 85–1,001.

94   'Give me your children!' Chaim Rumkowski's speech, Lodz, 4 September 1942, in Henryk Ross, Thomas Weber, Martin Parr, and Timothy Prus, *Lodz Ghetto Album* (New York: Chris Boot, Archive of Modern Conflict, 2005), 148–9.

95   See <http://kehilalinks.jewishgen.org/lodz/statistics.htm#Western>

96   Norbert Troller 'Introduction', in *Theresienstadt: Hitler's Gift to the Jews* (University of North Carolina Press, 1991), xxi.

97   Ibid., xxxii.

98   Between 430,000 and 500,000 Jews were murdered at Bełżec, along with an unknown number of Poles and Roma. Only 7 Jews imprisoned at the camp survived, which is the main reason why Bełżec is so little known despite its large number of victims. In addition, 200,000 to 300,000 or more Jews – taken from Poland, France, Germany, Holland, Czechoslovakia, and the Soviet Union and including Soviet prisoners of war – died in Sobibór.

99   Mark Smith, *Treblinka Survivor: The Life and Death of Hershl Sperling* (Stroud, England: The History Press, 2010).

100 Gitta Sereny, *The German Trauma: Experiences and Reflections 1938–2000* (London: Allen Lane, Penguin, 2000).

101 Silesia is a mining region in south-west Poland.

102 Christopher Andrew, *The Defence of the Realm: The Authorized History of MI5* (London: Penguin Books, 2010), 3.

103 Ibid., 129.

104 Ibid., 220.
105 Brinson and Dove, *Matter of Intelligence*, 2.
106 Anything marked with two asterisks (**) is a factual inaccuracy
107 After a Jewish funeral, the immediate family return home to sit *shiva*, a seven-day period of mourning. The week is referred to as 'sitting shiva' and is intended as an emotionally and spiritually healing time when family gather together, sit on low seats and are visited by friends and relatives, often bringing gifts of food.
108 Gaby Weiner '"We are decent people; only we had to pay a very high price, not to hurt the other people concerned": Three lives in a letter', in Andrew C. Sparkes (ed.) *Auto/Biography Yearbook 2012* (Durham: Auto/Biography Study Group, Russell Press, 2013), 48–60.
109 London, *Whitehall and the Jews 1933–1948*.
110 Ibid., 274.

Lightning Source UK Ltd.
Milton Keynes UK
UKOW01f0035240916

283702UK00003B/16/P